"High Hills"

There is much comfort in high hills,
and a great easing of the heart.
We look upon them,
and our nature fills with loftier images
from their life apart.
They set our feet on curves of freedom,
bent to snap the circles of our discontent.
Mountains are moods,
of larger rhythm and line,
moving between the eternal mode and mine.
Moments of thought,
of which I too am part,
I lose in them my instant of brief ills.
There is a great easing of the heart,
and cumulance of comfort on high hills.

— Geoffrey Winthrop Young

The poet was a famous alpine mountaineer and
President of the Alpine Club 1941-44

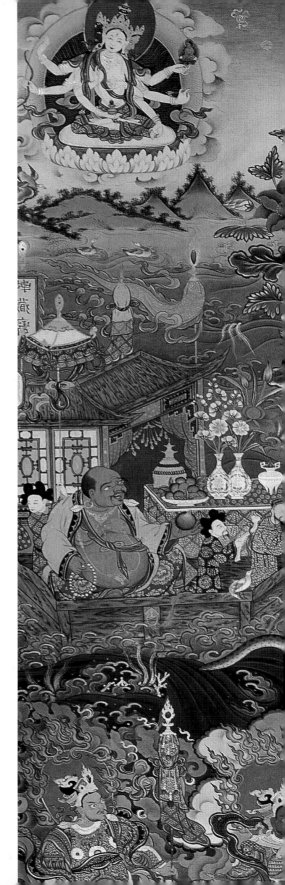

Published by
PERMANENT BLACK
D-28 Oxford Apartments,
11, I.P. Extension,
New Delhi 110092

Distributed by
ORIENT LONGMAN LTD
Bangalore Bhubaneshwar
Calcutta Chennai
Ernakulam Guwahati
Hyderabad Lucknow
Mumbai New Delhi Patna

Edited by Anuradha Roy
Design and layout by
Neelima Rao

Colour Separations,
Thomson Press, New Delhi
Printed and bound by
CS Graphics, Singapore

Photograph pages:
*(2-3) Siniolchu and Kangchendzonga at dawn
from the Rest Camp en route to Green Lakes in
the Zemu valley.*

*(4-5) Magnolia blossoms in the spring near the
village of Tsokha against a backdrop of
Pandim, Narsing and Jobonu. Tsokha is the
customary first night stop on the Dzongri/
Goecha La trek.*

*(6-7) Women pray at Tashiding monastery
during the Bumchu festival.*

*(8-9) Young lamas watch the masked dances at
Enchey monastery in Gangtok.*

Sikkim

A Traveller's Guide

Photographs and
Essays by Sujoy Das

Text by Arundhati Ray

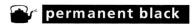
permanent black

For my grandmother
who introduced me to the Himalaya

Contents

Clouds cover the peaks of Narsing and Jobonu as seen from the Dzongri maidan after heavy spring snowfall

The Five Treasures of
the Great Snows

· ·

" A distant view of a snowy range.. has a strange power
of moving all poets and persons of imagination"

Round Kanchenjunga by Douglas Freshfield

I was eight years old when I first saw Mount Kangchendzonga, guardian
deity of the Sikkimese, from the hill-station of Darjeeling in West Bengal.
Floating high over the cloud-covered lower Himalaya, she towered over
the town, her summit reaching for the heavens. She was surrounded by her
attendant peaks, Jannu, Kabru, Ratong, Pandim and Siniolchu, all giants in
their own right, but, eclipsed by the grace and majesty of Kangchendzonga.
Though the mountain was situated on the Sikkim-Nepal border, some 74
kilometres from Darjeeling, the snows seemed close enough to touch.

Our family has spent many holidays in the mountains. As a child, I
would accompany my grandmother to Darjeeling where we had a house.
Our holiday was punctuated with long walks in the hills and views of the

Kangchendzonga range from different parts of the town. My grandmother told me about early mountaineering exploits on the peak and its ultimate conquest in 1955 by a team of British mountaineers. The expedition had stopped a few metres short of the summit in deference to the wishes of the Chogyal of Sikkim who did not want the sacred mountain violated. She spoke of the Singalila ridge of Phalut and Sandakphu from where the mountain was visible at "hand-shaking" distance, of the Green Lake Plain in North Sikkim on the Zemu Glacier where the mirror image of the mountain was reflected in a lake of emerald waters.

I saw the mountain in her various moods. Burnished copper at dawn, slowly changing to pink, gold and then dazzling white. More often than not, clouds would rush in and the "snows" as they were referred to in Darjeeling, would be blanketed out in thick mist.

We often went walking on a misty afternoon towards the neighbouring village of Ghoom, past window boxes ablaze with geraniums and begonias. Ghoom was notorious for its pea-soup of a fog and I used to gaze through the "white out" imagining a snow storm or blizzard raging on the mountain. Sometimes, if we were lucky, the weather would improve and a ridge or flank of Kangchendzonga would appear for an ever so brief moment and then vanish again into the mists. Between Darjeeling and Kangchendzonga a sea of clouds submerged Sikkim, an independent kingdom in those days, hiding it from view. I started to read all the available literature about the mountain. I read about the

travels of the British botanist, Sir Joseph Dalton Hooker who came to collect plants in 1849 and took the Sikkim rhododendron back to Kew Gardens in London. The explorer Douglas Freshfield's reconnaissances in 1899 and the accounts by the surveyors Pandit Sarat Chandra Das of his visit to Tibet in 1879 and Rinzing of his crossing of the Jonsangla in 1884 made heady reading. I read about the Lepchas, the original inhabitants of Sikkim, who called the mountain 'Kong-lo-chu' or 'The Highest Screen or Curtain of the Snows' and their worship of Kangchendzonga through the Pang Lhabsol dances.

As I visited Darjeeling year after year, the urge to get closer to the mountain became irresistible. I started out by making short trips to the Singalila ridge, a two day walk from Darjeeling, but, this merely whetted my appetite. Kangchendzonga seemed to have an inexorable hold on me. I wanted to photograph the mountain from all angles, in all seasons. I wanted to travel to the four sacred caves of Sikkim, high in the mountains where the lamas worshipped Kangchendzonga every year. I wanted to experience the festivals of Pang Lhabsol, Bumchu and Kagyet enacted in the sacred monasteries. I wanted to travel amongst the people who lived in the shadow of the mountain—the Bhutias, the Lepchas,

In 1978, I made my first visit to the mountains of the Sikkim Himalaya. It was early November and I was bound for the monastery of Pemayangtse, perched on a hill-top 2100 meters high in Western Sikkim, the cradle of its Buddhism. Pemayangtse is the royal monastery whose lamas preside over all palace functions. It is the principal monastery in Sikkim of the Nyingma-pa (red-hat) sect of Buddhists. I started out from the hill town of Kalimpong in West Bengal in the morning, hoping to reach Pemayangtse by nightfall. As luck would have it, I missed the connecting bus from Jorethang and had to reach Gayzing, the district headquarters of West Sikkim, in the back of a lorry carrying grain.

It was dusk as the lorry entered Gayzing, the sky heavily overcast. A blustery wind blew across the valley indicating snow in the mountains. Pemayangtse was five kilometres away, a steep climb of about an hour. No transport was available at that hour of the evening, so I decided to walk up—determined to capture the early morning sun on film.

The first drops of rain began to fall as I left the squat lights of Gayzing and headed up a narrow trail — the short cut to Pemayangtse which locals claim saves thirty minutes! It drizzled most of the way and I reached the dak bungalow chilled to the bone. A surprised chowkidar was summoned from his quarters and asked to light a fire immediately. I stood on the verandah of the bungalow, relieved to be dry and warm and gazed at the rain over the valleys to the north. A few lights of the village of Yoksam broke the darkness. I retired for the night tired and despondent—it looked like the day's effort had been wasted and there was little hope for a clear view in the morning.

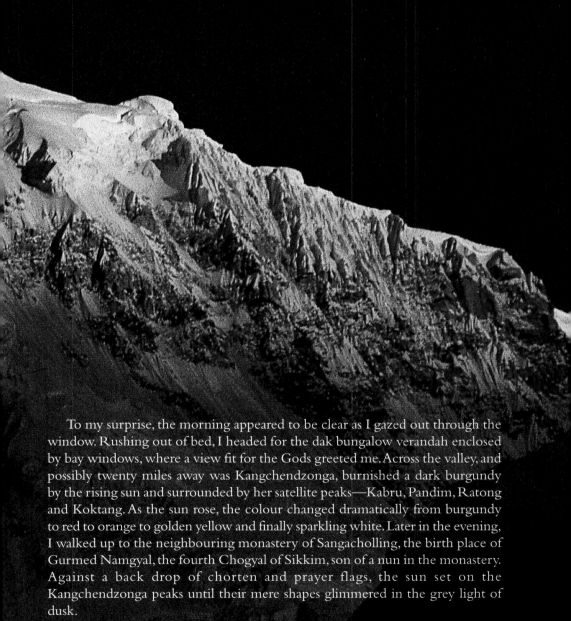

To my surprise, the morning appeared to be clear as I gazed out through the window. Rushing out of bed, I headed for the dak bungalow verandah enclosed by bay windows, where a view fit for the Gods greeted me. Across the valley, and possibly twenty miles away was Kangchendzonga, burnished a dark burgundy by the rising sun and surrounded by her satellite peaks—Kabru, Pandim, Ratong and Koktang. As the sun rose, the colour changed dramatically from burgundy to red to orange to golden yellow and finally sparkling white. Later in the evening, I walked up to the neighbouring monastery of Sangacholling, the birth place of Gurmed Namgyal, the fourth Chogyal of Sikkim, son of a nun in the monastery. Against a back drop of chorten and prayer flags, the sun set on the Kangchendzonga peaks until their mere shapes glimmered in the grey light of dusk.

From the monastery of Pemayangtse to the grazing alp of Dzongri is a three day walk. Through my years in Sikkim, Dzongri became one of my favourite places and I visited it no less than five times. One of my visits was at the height of the monsoon in 1988. I was accompanied by a friend from Calcutta and Mare Bhutia, an enterprising young porter from Yoksam, which is the last village on the road to the mountains. We walked through the Prek Chu valley, particularly torturous at this time of the year. The luxuriant mountain vegetation compensated for the hot and humid leech-infested trail. Gigantic tree ferns covered the valley floor and epiphytic orchids clung precariously to the branches of the tallest

Kabru as seen from the HMI Base Camp at Chauringkhang on a November morning.

rhododendrons. It drizzled steadily as we made our way through the fern-clad forest crouched beneath our umbrellas.

We stopped for the night at the dak bungalow of Bakhim that commands an extensive view over the valleys to the south. The next day we were en route to Dzongri, relieved to be out of the leech belt and savouring the cool air of the upper Himalaya.

Dzongri, situated at an altitude of 4000 metres, is a broad maidan below the peaks of Kangchendzonga and provides ideal summer grazing for sheep and yaks. The monsoon must be the most beautiful time on the alp. The weather is mild and the grass green and fresh. Numerous wild flowers including potentellias, saxifrage, anemones and primulas spread in a colourful patchwork and sheep and yaks graze contentedly on the luxuriant vegetation. The mountains are at their tantalizing best—a sharp shower and the clouds lift for a few minutes to reveal the steep south face of Pandim. Sometimes at dawn the sky is clear and the entire chain of peaks is visible, only to be blanketed out by thick rain clouds by mid-morning.

Resting on the thick grass I watched a distant figure loping over the meadow. As he drew closer, I realized that it was Chewang Bhutia, a yak herdsman who had accompanied me on an earlier visit to Dzongri. Chewang greeted me with a cheery wave and sat down to enjoy a cup of Tibetan tea brewed at a nearby yak hut. His yaks were grazing at the lake of Samiti, two days north of Dzongri. He was returning to his village, Yoksam, for further provisions and supplies.

As night fell, Chewang left for his village. We watched the Tibetan mastiffs herding the sheep and yaks to their pens for the night. Fires were lit in the yak huts and chang was brewed for the shepherds returning from the meadows. In the background, the clouds were a dazzling spectacle with the peaks sombre and majestic, floating into them with their everchanging patterns and hues. Far away in the valley below flashes of lightning were visible.

'It is raining at Yoksam,' said Mare Bhutia, pointing to his village 2100 metres below.

As we watched, the cloud cover from the valley began to rise like a fleecy white carpet and in a few moments we were covered by the damp mist. The yak huts glimmered in the distance and the first drops of rain greeted us as we returned to the Dzongri bungalow.

The base camp of Kangchendzonga in North Sikkim is situated on the Green Lake plain on the Zemu Glacier a few days walk from the roadhead at Lachen. The Zemu Glacier with an altitude of 5150 metres at it's head is surrounded by an array of snow capped peaks of which Kangchendzonga and Siniolchu are the most famous. The Zemu valley forms the approach to the north-eastern spur of Kangchendzonga, and was attempted, though unsuccessfully, by enterprising Bavarian expeditions lead by Paul Bauer once in 1929 and again in 1931. The British explorer Douglas Freshfield had travelled to Green Lakes along with the famous Italian photographer Vittorio Sella who had photographed Siniolchu from the Zemu valley. Freshfield had described Siniolchu as 'the most superb triumph of mountain architecture and the most beautiful snow mountain in the world'.

The approach march to Green Lakes takes around four days from the village of Lachen. The route follows the valley of the Zemu and culminates in the upper reaches of the Zemu Glacier. In summer, the Sikkim rhododendron is at its best and between altitudes of 3,000 and 4,000 metres, the valley is an explosion of colour. Most of the high altitude flowers like the Himlayan blue poppy, primulas and anemones, are in full bloom, along with the scarlet rhododendron. On a sunny day, with the peaks in full view and the flowers at their feet, this must be one of the finest walks in the Himalaya.

During the summer of 1987, I finally made it to Green Lakes. My trek there coincided with the Assam Rifles expedition to Kangchendzonga led by Major General Kukreti. When I reached their Base Camp, a two member team were high on the mountain ready to make the final push for the summit. The General was checking the daily weather reports from All India Radio, specially relayed for the expedition. After a good meal at their Base Camp, I retreated to the Rest Camp further down the valley to try and photograph Siniolchu in moonlight.

It was the full moon night of Buddha Purnima when I reached the Rest Camp. The weather had been clear for most of the day but as the sun set, clouds began to funnel their way up the valley from the east. In a few moments, most of the peaks were covered and the heavy mist reduced visibility to a few yards.

I dozed off to sleep in my tent setting the alarm for midnight in the hope that the clouds would lift by then. At the appointed hour, the shrill ring of the alarm bell shattered the silence, but a glance outside the tent was enough to establish that visibility remained the same as before.

I decided to sit up for the rest of the night at the entrance of my tent hoping for a break in the weather. It was bitterly cold as I donned all my warm clothing and sat covered by my sleeping bag. The ground outside the tent had frosted over and the valley was uncannily dark and sinister in the half glow of the moon.

I must have dozed off for some time for when I awoke the clouds were lifting. It was four in the morning and the moon had almost dropped behind the range of peaks which were now visible through the rapidly dissipating cloud cover. As I began to photograph, the clouds lifted over Siniolchu revealing a perfect pyramid, celestial in the moonlight. The sky gradually became brighter and a golden light bathed the mountains—the false sunrise. In the distance, the north-east spur of Kangchendzonga stood out—towering above her sister peaks. The light changed and changed again, as I watched mesmerised and continued photographing. At last satisfied, I perched myself on a rock and waited for the morning sun to bring warmth and happiness—another long cold Himalayan night was over.

Sikkim Himalaya

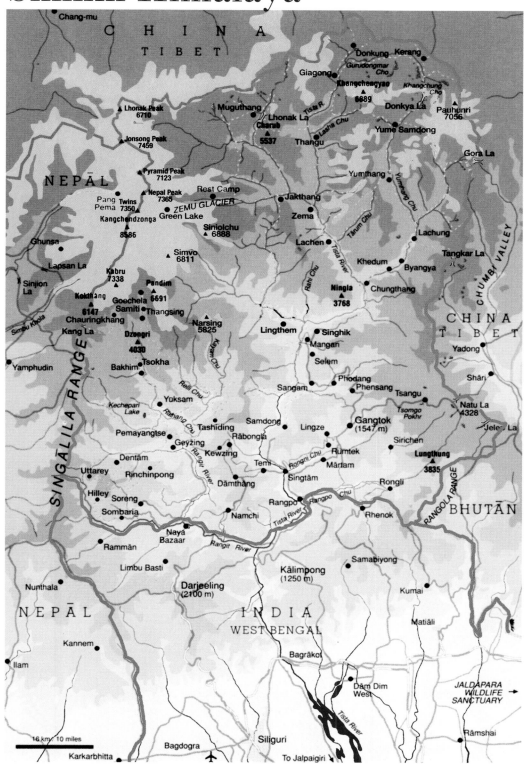

"Maro aryum mak, gong, talyang, sachuk, lavo, sahor,
punbyong nun–tuk rezang gum"
— The death of a good person is like the cloud covering up
the sun, moon and the stars

A Lepcha Saying

A Brief History of Sikkim

The original inhabitants of Sikkim were the Lepchas. The Lepchas have no written records, but their rich heritage of colourful legends and imaginative myths help to reconstruct their past. This oral tradition talks of various Lepcha chieftains going back to 1400 AD when Tur-ve Pa-no ruled the land.

It was in the fifteenth century, during the rule of the Lepcha chief Thekung Tek, that the first major migration of the Tibetan Kham people into Sikkim took place. Legend has it that a mighty Kham king, Kye Bhumsa, and his wife, remained childless for many years and were at last advised by the lamas to seek the advice of Thekung Tek, who had the reputation of being a seer. Accordingly, Kye Bhumsa, with a small group of followers, crossed the Yak-la and Penlong mountains and reached Sat-la near Rangpo. Bearing many gifts, he sought the audience of Thekung Tek in his dwelling in the deep jungles. He was told that he would father three sons. In due course this prophecy came true. A blood-brotherhood was sworn between Kye-Bhumsa, his sons, and Thekung Tek and his wife. With this, the Lepchas agreed that the Bhutias could settle in Sikkim and the two tribes would live harmoniously as friends. The Lepcha chief erected nine stones facing Mount Kangchendzonga at Kabi to mark the pact and invoked all the guardian deities of Sikkim as witnesses. The nine stones marking the first pact between the Lepchas and the Bhutias still stand at Kabi Longstok and to this day the Sikkimese celebrate the anniversary of the pact on the fifteenth day of the ninth month of the Tibetan calendar.

Kye Bhumsa's second son, Mipon-Rab, settled in Gangtok. His Tibetan kinsmen inter-married with the local Lepcha population and despite the agreement that the two groups should enjoy perfect parity, the settlers were soon the dominant power and their religion, Buddhism, gradually began establishing its hegemony over the entire population.

The consolidation of the Bhutias' superior position in Sikkim occurred with the crowning of Mipon-Rab's son, Phuntsog Namgyal, as the King of Sikkim in 1642. According to Sikkim lore, three lamas travelling along different mountain paths convened at Yoksam in West Sikkim. The triumvirate debated the need for Sikkim to have a temporal and spiritual head who would actively propagate Buddhism among the people. Messengers were then sent to Gangtok to summon Phuntsog Namgyal to Yoksam. And at Yoksam, he was consecrated by the learned priests as the first Chogyal of Sikkim.

THE CHOGYALS OF SIKKIM

The most notable Chogyal was the third Chogyal, Chador Namgyal. He was born of a Tibetan mother and ascended the throne in 1700 when he was only fourteen.

His coronation was bitterly opposed by his half-sister, Pedi Wangmo, whose mother came from Bhutan. She conspired to have him assassinated with the help of Bhutanese troops. Anticipating this, a loyal minister spirited the King away to Lhasa and put him in the care of the Dalai Lama. The young King grew up in an atmosphere of learning and religion and distinguished himself as a brilliant scholar.

Meanwhile, Bhutanese troops occupied the palace at Rabdentse as well as large tracts of the lower valleys. It was only after eight years, with pressure from the Dalai Lama, that they withdrew. Chador Namgyal returned and began ruling from Rabdentse. Founding the monastery at Pemayangtse, he ordered that the second of every three sons in a Bhutia family take monastic orders. The Lepcha script, and the warrior dance performed to this day during the worship of the mountains are both said to be his creations.

The ceremonial procession leaves the palace for the coronation of Chogyal Palden Thondup Namgyal

A WEDDING OF TWO WORLDS

When Hope Cooke, a graduate of the exclusive Sarah Lawrence College in Bronxville, New York, came to Darjeeling for a holiday in 1959, she could not have dreamt that her life as a Manhattan debutante was going to change forever. But it did. In Darjeeling she met the widowed Crown Prince of Sikkim, Palden Thondup Namgyal. Palden Thondup himself had become the Crown Prince because of an accident of fate: born as the second son he was training to head a lamasery until the death of his elder brother in an air crash made him heir to the throne. Hope and Palden fell in love, and decided to marry. The date was fixed by astrologers who deemed that the portents were not auspicious for 1962; the wedding was delayed till the following year. It was finally on 20 May 1963, that Hope Cooke became Hope Namgyal, the future Gyalmo of Sikkim.

Song composed especially for the American bride:
Today in the capital of Sikkim
Land of the East,
A flower of the West
Blossoms amongst us.
A daughter of Eve,
the great mother
Has come to this
land of Sikkim.
All friends who have
come to this
Royal wedding,
join us in our
Rejoicing.

The wedding was held at the royal family's temple on the palace grounds. The wedding was conducted according to Buddhist rites and no ritual was overlooked in the transformation of the young American girl into Sikkim's future queen. On the morning of the nuptials, the bridegroom's party met the bride and her attendants, exchanged khadas and sipped butter-tea with them. Later, the court astrologer traced auspicious symbols on the bride's fingertips with an inkless gold pen to protect her from evil forces and to ensure for her a happy marriage and prosperity. The wedding began with the wedding song and the bridal party entered the temple to the bellowing of ten-foot horns, the clash of cymbals, the roll of drums. Lamas conducted the ceremony, assisted by attendants whose birth-dates and horoscopes were in harmony with those of the bride and bridegroom. The Prince's father, Chogyal Tashi Namgyal sat watching from his high golden throne. At last, the bride, draped in white ceremonial dress, mounted to the altar to light the sacred lamps. Khadas were exchanged between the betrothed and the wedding was over.

After the solemn and dignified ceremony, came the celebrations, as the kingdom welcomed its brand-new princess. Folk dances greeted the newlyweds as they left the temple. Hundreds of Sikkimese and visitors besieged the temple to present the Prince and his bride with gifts of gold, silver, cloth, fruits, spices and bales of yak-hair—whatever they could afford. Thousand of silk scarves lay in shimmering heaps on the floor.

Over 5,000 guests had been invited: nobles and farmers, diplomats and yak herdsmen, generals and traders. Nepal, Bhutan and India sent contingents of guests. Refugees from Chinese-held Tibet arrived, as did 2,000 visitors from the West. Twenty cooks had to prepare a gargantuan feast to feed the entire party.

All along, Chador Namgyal's half-sister was busy with her evil machinations. She finally succeeded in having the Chogyal assassinated by a Tibetan surgeon during a royal bath in the hot springs. The murderous doctor was executed soon after; and in a manner befitting royalty, the princess was dispatched as well by strangling her with a scarf made of the finest silk. The Namgyal dynasty continued to rule.

By the end of the eighteenth century, the Namgyals were firmly established as the uncontested rulers of Sikkim. Not surprisingly, the aristocracy in Sikkim was strongly influenced by the court culture of Tibet, and most Chogyals chose their wives from Tibet. Over time, Lepchas increasingly adopted Buddhism and the two groups became more and more integrated. There was no racial conflict between them and when, in the eighteenth and nineteenth centuries, Bhutanese and Nepalese forays into Sikkim greatly increased in frequency, Lepchas and Bhutias joined forces against these common enemies. The ties between the two groups were thereby further cemented.

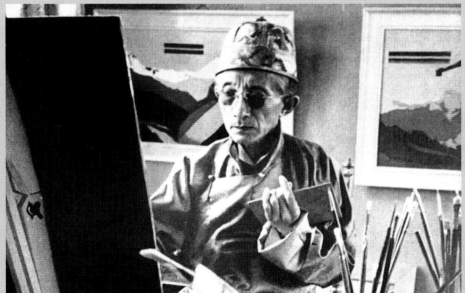

Chogyal Tashi Namgyal, a gifted painter

ENTER, THE BRITISH

The extensive infringement upon Sikkim's territorial borders by the Bhutanese and the Nepalese led to the loss of Limbuana to the Nepalese in the early eighteenth century and Kalimpong to the Bhutanese in the latter part of the same century. It also provided the British with a long-desired opportunity for political manouvering. Sikkim had sought British aid against the Gurkha invasions from Nepal. The British obliged. The Gurkhas were driven out of the Terai and the territories restored to Sikkim under the Treaty of Titaliya in 1817. Under this treaty, however, the British assumed the role of lords paramount in Sikkim.

Inexorably, Sikkim lost more and more territory to the British, including the beautiful hill-station of Darjeeling. But the biggest blow came in 1861 when the British government was given the power to build a road through Sikkim and the Jelep La to the Chumbi Valley and Lhasa. This was done to facilitate British trade.

Along with territorial acquisitions, the British consolidated their position in Sikkim by encouraging a huge influx of Nepalese people, despite the Chogyal's opposition to this policy. Small numbers of Nepalese had been migrating to Sikkim from about the fifteenth century, but it was only with the British that the Nepalese began entering in great numbers, entirely upsetting the traditional ethnic balance of Sikkim. This social engineering was done by the British to reduce the proportion of Lepchas and Bhutias in the total population with British imperial interests required a weakening of Lepcha-Bhutia strength. The British could also rest with the certainty that if the aristocracy of Sikkim showed any sign of protest, they could count on Gurkha support to quell rebellion.

LEPCHA LANGUAGE

The origins of the Lepcha language remain shrouded in mystery as philologists debate whether it belongs to the Tibeto-Burman group or the Austro-Asiatic family. The language is monosyllabic in character and possesses an inexhaustible capacity for derivatives and suffixes. Two striking aspects of the language are the wealth of vocabulary devoted to nature making it possible to verbalize complex subtleties of the natural world; and the allusive characteristic of the idiom, so that the language appears to revolve around innuendo and a verbal statement is almost always a suggestion rather than an explicit observation. Not surprisingly, this has made the Lepcha language rich in metaphors, similes and riddles and, consequently, very poetic. It is now generally accepted in the eighteenth century the third Chogyal Chador Namgyal created a script for the Lepchas based on the Tibetan alphabet.

At the turn of the century a Sikkim secretariat was established. Sidkeong Tulku was now the Chogyal. He was a powerful personality, highly intelligent, and with an Oxford education. He assumed a number of ministerial positions in the Sikkim government. Even before he became the Chogyal in 1914, he had made it clear that he intended to introduce large-scale reforms, including the abolition of the landlord system. Not surprisingly, this made him quite a few formidable enemies and his untimely death, within a few months of his having being crowned Chogyal, is widely regarded as an assassination.

Tashi Namgyal succeeded his brother Sidkeong and the fifty years of his reign saw many political and economic reforms. He was an excellent diplomat and established friendly working relations with the British. As a result, the British gave him considerable support in implementing various developmental programmes. The most spectacular of these was Tashi Namgyal's literacy drive which led to schools being opened in even the most remote areas of Sikkim and education becoming freely available to all. He ushered in an era of welfare and broad-based progress in which there was great emphasis on the development of human resources.

Meanwhile, his son, Palden Thondup Namgyal, having completed his training with the Indian Administrative Service, emerged as the Chogyal's main advisor in the judicial and executive affairs of Sikkim. Consequently, when Tashi Namgyal died in 1963, and Palden ascended the throne, he was already a seasoned minister with twenty years of administrative experience behind him. Under his direction the programme for development gained momentum — there were new roads, bridges, schools, hospitals, government institutions and housing, more transport and hydroelectric power.

ENTER, INDIA

With the departure of the British from the Indian sub-continent in 1947, the newly formed Republic of India inherited Sikkim as a protectorate. Chogyal Tashi Namgyal and, later, Chogyal Palden Thondup continued to maintain friendly relations with the newly formed Indian government. But trouble was brewing in Sikkim as various political groups, perhaps influenced by the political euphoria and excitement prevalent in India, began agitating for democratic processes to be instituted in the state. Political parties started springing up and the demand for people's power looked to threaten the monarchy.

On 1 May 1949, Sikkim's first popular ministry was formed under the Chief Ministership of Tashi Tshering. This five-member council was assigned executive powers but soon there was a feeling of dissatisfaction about the ministers' ability to actually exercise their powers. This led to more unrest and finally to large-scale riots in front of the palace gates in June 1949. The Chogyal had to take the help of Indian forces to quell the riots and this ultimately led to the Indo-Sikkim Treaty being signed on 5 December 1950. According to this agreement India assumed total responsibility of Sikkim's defence. Indian troops were stationed in Sikkim and the country's arms imports, foreign policy and passport matters were to be regulated by the Indian government. Roads and communications in Sikkim also came under the exclusive purview of India.

Meanwhile, as the demands for greater people's power continued, the Chogyal and representatives of two of Sikkim's largest parties, the Sikkim State Congress and the Sikkim National Party, held discussions and as a result, in May 1951, the Parity Formula was evolved. According to this formula, the seats in the proposed state council were to be divided equally between the Bhutia-Lepcha group, and the Nepalese. The Sikkim State Council was then instituted in 1953.

Even as internal instability continued with the Nepalese and the Bhutia-Lepcha nexus persisting in their battle to gain the upper-hand in the country's politics, Indian forces clashed with China on the kingdom's northern borders in October 1962 and the Chogyal was forced to declare a state of emergency in the country. The following year Chogyal Tashi Namgyal died. The Crown Prince, Palden Thondup was crowned the twelfth Chogyal and his American wife, Hope Cooke, the Gyalmo.

In April 1973, the trouble which had been brewing between the Lepcha-Bhutia factions and the majority Nepalese group, erupted into a political furore of riots. The Nepalese were demanding an election format of "one-man, one-vote". Once more, the Chogyal had to seek the help of India to restore order and thereafter an Agreement was signed whereby the Chogyal's status was further reduced. He now became virtually a titular head, real power having shifted into the hands of India and to the majority group. Kazi Lhendup Dorji, a man well-known for his anti-monarchist sentiments and his pro-India bias, was elected to the Council of Ministers.

After this, it was only a matter of time before Sikkim ceased to exist as an independent nation. It formally became a part of the Indian Republic in 1975 when Kazi Lhendup Dorji appealed to the Indian parliament for representation, and for

Sikkim to become an Indian state. India accepted. The three-hundred year-old institution of the Chogyal was declared abolished by a resolution passed in the Sikkim Assembly. On 16 May 1975, Sikkim became the twenty-second state of India with the Kazi as Chief Minister.

Sikkim's absorption into the Indian Union has remained a sensitive and controversial issue among the native Sikkimese population. At the time of the merger India had promised that Sikkim's integration with mainstream India would not threaten Sikkim's unique cultural identity. However, many Sikkimese believe that the decades following 1975 have witnessed a steady corrosion of this identity. They hold that the tiny state is now overrun by a disproportionately large bureaucracy which has, to quote a journalist, sullied this beautiful Himalayan region with "paan-stained babudom". The corruption afflicting the political machinery of the other Indian states is, in Sikkim, magnified many times over and it is popularly alleged that the so-called 'planned development' that the Indian government insists it is effecting in the state is just an euphemism for the destruction of Sikkim's environment and heritage by government officials and construction contractors. The Sikkimese solution to these problems would be far greater power in the hands of the Lepchas, Bhutias and the authentic Nepalese population of Sikkim so that the state is run by those truly belonging to it, with the interests of the state uppermost in their minds. Among the native population there is an agitation for far greater representation in the state's government and a more active role in administration and policy matters.

ECONOMY

Sikkim was part of the ancient trade route between Tibet and India with Gangtok a busy trade post. Yaks, mules and donkeys would come from Tibet laden with wool and return carrying precious stones, tobacco, dried fruit, sugar, molasses and many domestic items like needles and soap. This ancient form of livelihood has not survived, because of the sealing of the border with Tibet, but the other traditional economic sustenance of the people—agriculture—still dominates. Over seventy per cent of Sikkim's workforce is employed in agriculture-related activity. The terrace farms and plantations of Sikkim, lying in steps all along mountain sides, are fragrant with cash crops like cardamom, ginger, apricots, peaches and mandarin oranges. Both mandarins and cardamom are exported, Sikkim being one of the world's largest exporters of the spice. The Temi Tea Estate is the sole source of the state's recently-established tea industry but the leaves nurtured in this spectacularly beautiful garden located near Singtam fetch some of the highest prices in tea auctions the world over.

In the alpine regions, large numbers of Bhutias are yak herdsmen by profession. This is an ancient occupation and even today the herdsmen follow the transmigratory patterns of their ancestors, grazing their herds in the high altitudes in summer and moving down to their villages during winter. Yaks are ideal beasts of burden for rugged mountainous terrain. Their thick coats provide wool and the meat is dried and eaten. The rich and nutritious milk from yaks is used to make churpi, a cheese, and butter.

Less pastoral pursuits include assorted fruit preservation factories, mines, and breweries. Danny Dengzongpa, once a popular "Bollywood" villain whom Indian audiences loved to hate, produces Dansberg, a beer much consumed in India. Colourful, gimmicky time-pieces under the brand name "Hi-Funda" are manufactured as well.

The Government Institute of Cottage Industries, set up in 1957 by Chogyal Palden Thondup, develops handicrafts like silversmithing, carpet weaving, wood carving and hand-made paper. But in recent years, it is floriculture—given Sikkim's incredible range of orchids and other flowers—and tourism that have emerged as the two major sources of income for the state.

Sikkim is suffering the usual consequences of this rapid development. Large tracts of hill-side have been carved out for roads and mines; deforestation is extensive. This has led to severe reduction in the forest cover as well as soil erosion and, consequently, landslides are now a frequent hazard.

CHAMPAGNE OF TEAS

Temi Tea Estate located in South Sikkim is not only breathtakingly beautiful, the garden is also a producer of some of the world's best tea. The Chogyal had intiated tea growing in Sikkim with a small plantation in Kewzing to provide employment for the Tibetan refugees escaping Chinese aggression in their homeland. This was later moved to Temi and a proper processing plant constructed. This government-owned Estate produces about about 100,000 kg of tea annually which fetches premium prices at world auctions.

The hour-long drive from Singtam up to the Estate takes you through mountainsides lush with ferns and numerous waterfalls ranging from musical rills to roaring cascades cross your path as they rush downwards. Temi is planted on steep hillsides ranging from 1200 metres to 1800 metres and the road up to the factory, situated at 1500 metres is lined with cherry blossom trees which come into bloom in November. All of this verdant natural beauty seems to feed into the tea, giving it a uniquely subtle, multi-layered fragrance.

"Trees, water, stones:
Let these answer a gaze contemplative
Of all things that flow out from them
And back to enter them again."

—*Charles Brasch*

Of Mountains and Rivers

The north east face of Kangchendzonga from the base camp at Green Lakes

*N*ye-me-el, Paradise. This is what the Lepchas called Sikkim. And certainly, as every visitor finds out, it is among the most strikingly beautiful and unspoilt regions of the Himalaya. Within its 7300 square kilometres, Sikkim contains an amazing variation of altitude ranging from the southern foothills which rise only to about 305 metres to the towering heights of the Kangchendzonga massif at 8,586 metres. To the North, it is bordered by the Greater Himalayan range and the Tibetan Plateau, while to the West, the Singalila ridge forms a natural boundary with Nepal. The Chola mountains mark the eastern boundary, with the Chumbi Valley in the North-East and Bhutan in the South-East. And the Rangit river, its moods changing with the changing seasons, forms most of the southern border with West Bengal's Darjeeling district.

THE PEAKS

Kangchendzonga redefines mountains. Mont Blanc is the highest peak in Europe at 4,807 metres, Mount McKinley, the highest in North America at 6,194 metres, Kilimanjaro, the highest in Africa at 5,895 metres, Mount Cook, the highest in Australasia at 3,764 metres. If superimposed on Mount Kangchendzonga none of these would reach further than its Advance Base Camp!

In any Himalayan state, the mountains are naturally the prime geophysical features and Sikkim has a more than ten snow-capped peaks that soar above 6000 metres. But while giants like **Kabru** (7338 metres), **Pandim** (6691 metres) and **Siniolchu** (6888 metres) can all claim attention, it is Kangchendzonga, the world's third highest peak at a dizzying

8686 metres, that dominates the physical and psychological landscape of Sikkim.

Kangchendzonga's expanse of shimmering snow and rock is a conglomeration of five peaks. Its Tibetan name translates into Five Treasures of the Great Snows, an allusion to the Sikkimese belief that the mountain is the repository of the five holy items essential for life: minerals, grain, salt, weapons and the holy scriptures. It is revered throughout Sikkim as the guardian deity to which annual prayers are offered by both Buddhists and the Lepchas.

The mountainsides are honey-combed with caves and studded with lakes. And as if to emphasize the tremendous natural contrasts that are the hallmark of Sikkim, along with the freezing waters of the alpine lakes, there are numerous hot springs where

Kabru (left) and Kangchendzonga from the south as viewed from the monastery of Rinchinpong in West Sikkim. The town in the lower right hand of the frame is Gayzing with Pemayangtse monastery on the ridge above.

temperatures can touch 50°C. The land is irrigated by two main rivers, the Tista and the Rangit, which, along with their numerous tributaries, slice their way southwards, leaving behind them gorges and valleys along whose ridges

and slopes the population of Sikkim dwell.

Four of the innumerable caves that dot the Sikkim mountains are revered as places of pilgrimage. These **Four Great Caves** are considered to be the abodes of the Guru Rimpoche and Lhatsun Chenpo and are visited regularly by lamas. The most holy of these is **Laringvigphu** (literally, "the old cave of God's hill") in North Sikkim which can be reached after a three-day trek from Tashiding. To reach the "cave of happiness", **Dechenphu**, one must must trek to the rarified heights of Dzongri. **Pephu**, located in South Sikkim, is the "secret cave", lying between the Tendong and Maenam mountains, 5 kilometres away from Rabongla. The easiest cave to reach is **Kadosangphu**, the "cave of the fairies", located very close to the Rishi hot springs on the road to Pemayangtse monastery.

Most of Sikkim's caves are located in remote places, requiring arduous treks. But when you chance upon one of these caverns on a remote mountainside and step in to find the tiny flames of votive lamps left by a visiting lama lighting up the dark depths with their flickering lights, it can be an almost mystical experience, particularly if you are alone.

Where there are mountains, there are passes—the passage ways between towering ranges—crucial for travel and communications. Sikkim's passes are located at high altitudes and most of the major passes, being on sensitive border terrain, are now occupied by the army. Passes with musical names like **Chorten-nyima-la, Nathu-la, Jelep-la** and **Cho-la**, which were at one time important, oft-used corridors between Sikkim and Tibet are today inaccessible to non-military personnel. However, the Indian and Chinese governments are negotiating to revive the old trade routes linking Sikkim and Tibet and this could result in the opening up of the Nathu-la and Jelep-la passes.

Sunset over Mount Gurudongmar from Dorji La on the North Sikkim plateau

Overleaf: Cloud formations over the peaks of the Zemu valley

LAKES AND SPRINGS

Many of Sikkim's lakes are situated at high altitudes, embedded in rugged and steep mountain terrain. These expanses of water are usually small, and are icebound in winter. The North Sikkim plateau adjoining Tibet has a number of mountain lakes of which **Gurudongmar** and **Chho Lamo** are the most famous. Gurudongmar is an important place of pilgrimage for Sikhs, especially the soldiers who man the inhospitable border posts; Chho Lamo is widely regarded as the source of the Tista river. Other important lakes are **Khechoperri**, **Tsangu**, **Menmecho** and **Green Lake**.

In Sikkimese lore the beautiful **Khechoperrie** lake is the bride of Kangchendzonga. Situated at 1840 metres, a day's gruelling uphill trek from Yoksam, the lake lies secreted away in a forest of rhododendron. When windswept, the surface of the lake shimmers in patterns of turquoise and silver; on a still day the waters are like a stretch of azure

glass. So hallowed is the lake in local imagination that it is believed that even birds protect its sanctity by carrying away any leaf or twig that drifts on to the lake so its waters are not marred by a speck. Another local tradition holds that the lake's deity can grant the wish for a son and everyday hundreds of little lamps are floated on the surface, their flickering flames carrying the prayers of couples yearning for sons.

Along with lakes, Sikkim also has

numerous glaciers, many of which are the sources of rivers. Among these is the **Zemu**, which is the largest, while the **Rathong**, the **Talung**, the **Kabru** and the **Jonsong** are the other major glaciers. Goecha La, the final destination on the most popular trek in West Sikkim overlooks the Talung Glacier while the walk to Green Lake, the base camp of Kangchendzonga from the north-east, is along the Zemu glacier.

The sulphur waters of Sikkim's many hot springs are said to be very good for health. The **Yumthang** hot springs are located some distance away from Yumthang village amidst grazing pastures. You trek down the valley, and cross the Lachung Chu river, before finally reaching the baths. A 25 kilometre drive upstream from Yumthang through rhododendron country brings you to the **Yume Samdong** hot springs, located just at the base of the Donkia-la Pass.

Unlike the hot springs of North Sikkim, the **Phur-Cha-Chu** sulphur baths located near the small township of Rishi, are situated outdoors. This spa, which has to be approached over a footbridge fjording the Rangit river, is a Nepalese favourite: they have great faith in the medicinal properties of the waters.

RIVERS

Sikkim has two main waterways, the Tista and the Rangit, both of which are formed at high altitudes, partly from the melt of glaciers, partly from the drainage of alpine lakes. After this they are fed by the abundant monsoon rainfall. Both the Tista and the Rangit take serpentine routes in a generally southern direction, carving out deep valleys till they reach the state's southern boundary. The Rangit flows east and the Tista flows west, converging at the confluence near Melli.

The source of the **Tista** is the resplendent lake Chho Lamo, though

A Sikkimese family bathe at a hot spring near Ralang in the South District. Hot springs in Sikkim are famed for the medicinal properties of their waters.

some scholars believe that its true origins lie in the glacier Tista Khangse, a little further to the east of the lake. Two rivers, the Goma Chhu and the Naku Chhu, combine with the Zemu Chhu, and this combined force, cascading down, merges with the Tista 3 kilometres above Lachen. The Lachung Chu, a river that follows the Lachung valley, meets the Tista at Chungthang. The now powerful river hurtles through the gorges and steep valleys, its thunderous roar audible over considerable distances. At Mangan, the river is joined by the Talung Chu. At Singtam it widens to become double its width and, for the first time in its course, it is navigable. During the dry season rafting is possible between Singtam and Rangpo. From Rangpo the river bends in a south-westerly direction, and serves as a natural border with the state of West Bengal. At its confluence with the Rangit near Melli, the sight of its translucent jade waters merging with verdant forests is a spectacular sight. The currents are once again swift, the waters rough, throwing up surf and spray where they strike giant boulders. Rapidly passing the sleepy town of Tista, past the Coronation Bridge which is the access to Bhutan, on through the state of Assam, the Tista eventually flows into Bangladesh where it merges with the great Brahmaputra.

The **Rangit** traces its source to the Rathong glacier in West Sikkim. Like the Tista, its descent is sharp and swift and it is fed by many tributaries, the principle of these being Ramam Khola, Reli Chhu, Rathong Chhu and Rishi Khola. It travels through deep forests near the Pemayangtse monastery and Yoksam, and bifurcates the twin townships of Naya Bazar and Jorethang. From here the gradient eases and the river turns eastward dividing the lush forested foothills of Sikkim in the north from the tea estates of West Bengal in the south.

The Tista rushes through the gorge at Thangu in North Sikkim with pink rhododendrons in bloom

A Lepcha Tale of the Two Rivers

In ancient times, two river spirits—the God, Rangit and the Goddess Tista—lived in happiness in the lap of the Himalayas. One day they playfully challenged each other to a race down to the plains to see who flowed faster. Tista took as her guide the snake king who moved straight as an arrow down to the plain. But Rangit chose to follow the bird king who meandered and stopped at every distraction and took a long time to reach the plains. Finally when Rangit reached a precipice he sighted his beloved Tista waiting patiently for him, having reached much earlier. Ashamed to have lost the race, he threatened to overflow his banks and cause a flood. But Tista implored him to desist and hearing her prayers, Rangit made his peace. The two lovers fell into a long embrace and flowed down to the plains jointly, never to part again. This explains to us why the two rivers follow such different courses.

Modern highrise buildings, Gangtok

Sikkim is divided for administrative purposes into four districts. Gangtok is the state capital and the head quarters of the densely populated Eastern District; Mangan is the headquarters of the sparsely populated Northern District, the largest in terms of area; Gayzing is the headquarters of the Western District; and Namchi, the administrative centre of the Southern District, the smallest of them all.

The state capital and Eastern District headquarters, **Gangtok**, is situated on a ridge running north to south. Homes facing east are treated to dawn breaking over the snows of the Chola range and the road to Nathu-la. The Enchey monastery, situated on a spur above the town, is the highest building on the ridge. The ridge is also the prettiest part of town and the most elite. The residence of the Governor, the Tashi Namgyal Academy, a prestigious public school, the Royal Palace, the White Memorial Hall, and Tashiling, the seat of the State Government, are all situated here. Below this the ridge descends in layers. Private houses and government bungalows dot this area with the Government Institute of Cottage Industries as a landmark. The layers continue down to the market place of Mahatma Gandhi Marg, and the Gangtok suburbs of Deorali and Tadong. At the lower levels it is crowded, with two or three storied buildings that seem on the verge of falling over one another,

clinging precariously to the mountain side. In this familiar urban chaos may be found the prerequisites of modern living: hotels, chemists, hospitals, the post office, shops, cinemas. The Institute of Tibetology, the premier institution for research in Tibetan religion, medicine, language and theological studies is situated at Deorali.

Rangpo, another important town in the Eastern District, is the entry point to the state. The town has a large market where buses usually pull up for refreshments. Most of the eating houses serve liquor, and Sikkim Distilleries is situated here. The Tista is at its widest in Rangpo. Two or three kilometres above the town is the Sikkim Mining Corporation.

Singtam, a small industrial town in the east, is a popular halting place for those *en route* to the Temi Tea Estate, Namchi or Gayzing. Singtam's main street is a long market place containing several eating houses. Board and lodging are available, but the services provided are minimal. The state's food preservation industry is located a few kilometres outside Singtam.

The North District headquarters, **Mangan**, is a small township 45 kilometres from Gangtok, above the east bank of the Tista on the North Sikkim Highway. Across the river and beyond the intervening mountains looms Kangchendzonga. Below it is the Lepcha sanctuary of Dzongu, a reserve established by the Chogyals to protect the vanishing tribe.

Mahatma Gandhi Marg, Gangtok

Mangan is the last stop before rugged, mountainous terrain takes over, and the eating houses and provision stores here give you a last chance to stock up.

On the west bank of the Tista is a monastery and across the Tista bridge is the hamlet of **Chungthang.** It is a small northern town situated at the confluence of the Tista and the Lachung Chu rivers. It has assumed some importance because of the increasing presence there of the Indian Army.

Immediately beyond Chungthang the road forks to the west; to the left it runs parallel to the Tista and 28 kilometres away is **Lachen**—a Bhutia settlement. This alpine village is set amidst apple orchards and tall prayer flags flutter against a backdrop of sheer, brooding cliffs. Yaks graze on the open scrub land, beyond which the swift currents of the Tista continue their tumultuous descent to the plains.

Some distance before the village is the 150-year old Lachen monastery which belongs to the Nyingmapa sect. Domestic architecture is typically Bhutia. Despite its remote location Lachen boasts a post office, a police station and a primary school.

Located 24 kilometres beyond Chungthang on the road that runs along the Lachung Chu river, **Lachung** nestles in a valley which is ablaze in spring with bursts of the rhododendrons and azaleas that characterize the flora of this region.

The remote village of **Yumthang** is 135 kilometres beyond Gangtok, beyond Chungthang and even Lachung, along the North Sikkim Highway. This village on a windswept plain has a number of hot springs just a little distance away. The spectacular road to Yumthang from Lachung is lined with deep forests of rhododendron. The only traffic you are likely to encounter are herds of yak.

The market place of Gayzing, the district headquarters of West Sikkim on a monsoon evening

The head quarters of the South District, **Namchi**, is a south-facing town located on top of a hill. You can see snow capped peaks from the grounds of the tourist bungalow. The market place is not very large but is renowned for its goldsmiths. By and large, the population of this town is Nepalese and the best time to visit is during the Dasai festival.

Melli is one of the entry points into Sikkim and is situated on the banks of the Tista river. A few miles out of town is the confluence of the Tista and the Rangit—a holy place for the Lepchas and the Nepalese. Yoksam Breweries is located on a hill near this town.

Gayzing, the headquarters of the West District, is a bustling township. It is an important tourist centre because of its proximity to the monasteries of Pemayangtse and Tashiding and the historical ruins of Rabdentse; it is also the starting point of some of the best trekking territory in Sikkim.

Gurkha march-past at the Governor's Gold Cup football final, Gangtok

The Lower Valleys

" Down in the valley, the valley so low, hang your head
over and hear the wind blow"

The district headquarters of Gayzing in Western Sikkim is typical of many Sikkim towns. It is surrounded by paddy fields and orange orchards. Higher up on the hillside, there are cardamom plantations. The town has a main square surrounded by shops and this is a meeting place for the populace.

It was at Gayzing that I first met N.D.Das. A Bengali from Calcutta, Das had settled down in Sikkim and had a job with the Information Department. His children spoke fluent Nepali and went to the local Kyongsa school near the town. On my first visit in 1978, Das had put me up in his house. On my subsequent trips, I used to visit his home very often. He was a mine of information on the district having lived there for many years, and I used to consult him on possible routes and accommodation. We had long discussions in the courtyard outside his house and he used to ask me about Calcutta, a city which he had not visited for many years. His house had a good view of the Rangit valley and the hills around Gayzing. It often felt strange, discussing the bustle and milieu of Calcutta in the calm and serenity of Sikkim's lower valleys.

Children walk to school near Gayzing against a backdrop of gathering monsoon clouds

The morning after the Bumchu festival - devotees at Tashiding monastery

Another good friend at Gayzing was Wangyal, known to the locals as Yap Maila. Yap Maila hailed from an aristocratic Lepcha–Bhutia family. He had property near the town and owned cardamom fields at Pemayangtse. He was always curious about my research and ready to help. On one visit I accompanied Yap Maila and his family to the hot springs of Tatopani on the banks of the Rangit near the town of Legship.

Legend has it, that the founder lama of Sikkim, Lhatsun Chenpo, meditated at four sacred caves in the four corners of the land. The South Cave, Kadosangphu, is located near the Tatopani hot springs and is a popular pilgrimage spot. The medicinal waters of the springs were supposed to be a panacea for a large number of ailments. I accompanied Yap Maila into the cave while the rest of his family plunged into the bubbling waters of the sulphur springs. Flickering butter lamps lit the cave and the smell of incense pervaded the air. Yap Maila performed his puja and chanted his mantras 'om mani padme hum'. Prayer flags hung all around the walls. As we came out of the cave, we spotted his children splashing noisily in a pool of water. His wife lay in a another pool, immersed upto her neck oblivious to the shindy around her.

About an hours' drive from the town of Legship is the monastery of Tashiding, regarded as being the holiest in Sikkim. It is built on a site where, legend has it, a rainbow emanating from Kangchendzonga terminated. It was a small 'Lakhang' built by Ngadak Sempa Chempo, who placed in it a pot of holy water blessed by him after he had performed the Mane Mantra prayers five billion times. The 'Lhakhang' was subsequently reconstructed into a full fledged monastery. Each year on the fifteenth day of the first Tibetan month, corresponding to around March, thousands of pilgrims come to Tashiding for a few drops of Bumchu (holy water) as fresh as the day it was placed in the Bumpa (holy container) three hundred years ago. They call it the Bumchu festival.

I later visited Tashiding during one of the Bumchu festivals. The monastery is situated on a hill above the village. As I walked up, I noticed that stalls had sprung up along the way selling every conceivable item from sweets and chocolates to jewellery and Tibetan medicines. There was a great deal of merry-making and fun and frolic. People poured in from different parts of Sikkim and after performing the initial prayers at the huge Tashiding mendang, settled down to wait for the holy water which would be distributed at three in the morning—the hour selected by the lamas as being most auspicious.

In 1992, I returned to Gayzing after a gap of four years. I wanted to make a pilgrimage to Khechoperrie, the lake of wishes. Alighting from the bus, I spotted Yap Maila beneath an umbrella in the market square. He invited me to his home and introduced me to Topzor Bhutia, from Tashiding village, who wanted to float butter lamps on the lake—the customary puja at Khechoperrie. The jeep was arranged and we agreed to leave the next day. In 1849, the British botanist Hooker had travelled to Khechoperrie and the local lama had floated a lamp for him: I felt a spectral bond with the Englishman in search of plants so long ago.

We passed by the Rimbi Hydel Project and started climbing for the lake. It was the month of August, impromptu waterfalls cascading across the road. The rivers were in full spate and the water-driven prayer wheels spun furiously by the roadside. Freshly planted paddy contrasted against the jade green hillside. The clouds became darker and darker as we climbed up, rain seemed imminent. The trail to the shore of the lake was overrun with ferns and creepers.

A Lepcha home in the village of Lingthem in the Lepcha sanctuary of Dzongu

Khechoperrie was situated in an amphitheatre surrounded by hills. It was a dead-end, an appropriate place for an ultimate wish. Jet black water, slate grey storm clouds, brooding hills and the veil of willows around: Khechoperrie was truly 'mystic wonderful'.

I asked Topzor how deep the lake was.

"Nobody knows," he replied cheerfully, " but, very deep," as he continued to concentrate on cutting his bamboo bark.

Topzor arranged the butter lamps on the bark. After lighting them, he gently released the boat onto the waters of the lake. With hardly any breeze, the makeshift boat bobbed merrily along the shore, the lamps burning brightly. As I photographed, I wished. And, in a timeless gesture of reverence, the Sikkimese kneeled down and said a silent prayer.

That evening in Gayzing, I dropped in to see my old friend, N. D. Das. He waved to me from his house as I walked in, but, for some reason he was communicating in sign language. As I sat with him, I managed to comprehend the whole story. He had suddenly lost his wife last year and the shock of her death had caused a stroke. He had lost his speech. His daughter came smiling in with cups of tea—their resilience in the face of this enormous tragedy astounded me. I thought back to old times in their house—full of fun and laughter. Das showed me a photograph of his wife and himself which I had taken many years ago. He had framed it and hung it up on the wall. This time he could not ask me about Calcutta so I told him instead. He listened with a smile on his face. That night in Gayzing, I was unable to sleep.

The next day I left for Gangtok by bus. The monsoon seemed to have temporarily retreated and it was bright and sunny. As we rattled down the hillside, every blade of paddy gleamed in the sunshine. We passed groups of children going to school. Construction workers were heading for their sites, anxious to begin work before the rains set in again. Red chillies were drying on the rooftops. Clothes were being washed and put out in the sun. It was a typical 'lower valleys' day.

In the spring of 1997 I passed through Gayzing. Winds of change had been sweeping through the state. Sikkim had suddenly become the most popular tourist destination in eastern India. Hoards of visitors in new 'Commander' jeeps rushed up to Pemayangtse monastery daily. The idyllic village of Pelling where I had stayed almost eighteen years ago in Sonam's house below the chorten now had more than fifteen hotels, most of them ugly concrete constructions, all of them packed with visitors. The peace and sanctity of the Pelling-Pemayangtse ridge was gone forever.

I met Yap Maila in the market place. He told me he wanted to convert his cardamom fields below Pemayangtse monastery into a resort hotel, exclusively for foreign tourists.

" It is on the trail to Tashiding and has a great view of Kangchendzonga. A lot of tourists pass that way now," he added.

"Do you think it's a good idea?" he asked.

I remained silent with a vision of a luxury hotel in the middle of Yap Maila's fragrant green cardamom fields.

Devotees float butter lamps at Khechoperrie lake in West Sikkim

Paddy fields at Martam near the monastery of Rumtek at the height of the monsoon

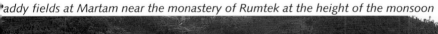

(Overleaf) Villagers winnow grain near the village of Singhik on an October afternoon
(Pages 52-53): Primulas bloom at the foot of the Lhonak-la pass, North Sikkim

"For epochs to come the peaks will still pierce the lonely vistas, but when the last snow leopard has stalked among the crags and the last markhor has stood on a promontory... a spark of life will have gone, turning the mountains into stones of silence"

Mountain Monarchs by George B Schaller

Rhododendrons bloom near the hot springs of Yume Samdong

Snow Leopards in the Mist

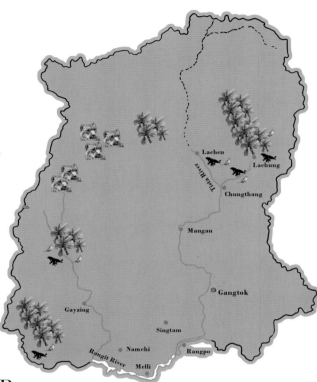

IN THE THREE BIOTOPES

Sikkim's considerable range of altitude and climatic conditions leads to immense variations in vegetation and wildlife. It has distinct climatic zones. Up to 1200 metres it is **tropical**: there are forests of tall shady trees like sal accompanied by a luxuriant undergrowth of shrubs. In these moist lowlands can be found canes, palms, bamboo, ferns and Sikkim's renowned orchids. The **temperate** zone, with its lofty oaks, maples, magnolias, birch and the conifers like fir and spruce stretches from 1200 metres to 3600 metres. Its bewildering variety of rhododendron ranges from shrubs at ground level to towering specimens that create the forest canopy. Above 3600 metres you enter an **alpine** zone. The vegetation here is low-lying and clustered, having evolved to survive in the bitter cold.

Trees are sparse, mainly juniper and pines, while grasses and sedge cover wide tracts. The shrubs and herbaceous plants that thrive in this area—gentians, geranium, blue poppies, even some dwarf rhododendron—stud the terrain with their brightly coloured flowers in spring.

The **rhododendron** is the breathtaking glory of Sikkim. There are about thirty species, varying in size, from the gigantic *Rhododendron grande*, a tree that can grow to 40 feet, down to the *Rhododendron nivale* which rises barely 2 inches from the ground. Some species like the Dalhousie are epiphytes growing on top of tall trees and are barely visible from the ground; others like the Falconeri are conspicuous with their large fleshy leaves covered with rust-coloured

NATIONAL PARKS

KANGCHENDZONGA NATIONAL PARK

Area: 850 square kilometres
Location: The Tent Peak and the ridge of the Zemu glacier are to its north; the ridge of Mt Lamo Angden to the east; in the south Mt Narsing and Mt Pandim and in the west the main peak of Kangchendzonga.
Altitude : 1600 metres to 8586 metres
Rivers: Talung Chu, Ratong Chu, Zemu Chu.
Major species: Snow Leopard, the Red Panda, the Himalayan Black Bear, Barking Deer, Tahr, Shapi, Tibetan wild ass, Clouded Leopard and Marbled Cat.

One of the highest mountain parks in the world, it includes the world's third highest peak. Because of its formidable location, the Park has remained untouched ecologically and provides natural protection to its fauna and flora. The extremely rugged mountain terrain with deep escarpments and plateaus in certain areas of the park are still not fully explored; and the possibility of discovering new species of flora and fauna in these regions cannot be ruled out. The Dzongri trek passes through the park.

filaments on their undersides. Extensive forests of rhododendron can be seen along the Singalila range, bordering the trail to Dzongri; and across large tracts of the Yumthang Valley. The highly coloured flowers of this plant have a crucial function: they are the only source of attraction for bees and butterflies since no species has any fragrance.

The other pride and joy of Sikkim is its **orchids**, of which 400 different kinds grow within Sikkim's boundaries. Orchids are concentrated between 1,200 to 2,200 metres but there are some varieties that do brave alpine terrain.

Sikkim's orchids belong to two categories: epiphyte and terrestrial; the epiphytes are better known and more

Orchids flower at the Gangtok flower show in April

numerous. The Dendrobium genus of epiphytic orchids is the most popular in Sikkim. Remarkable dendrobiums include the spectacular golden-yellow Hookerianas with its deeply-fringed lips and rich purple spots, and the large pouch-shaped Calceolaria in shades of white, pink and yellow. The Cristata species of the Coelogyne genus, which

Rhododendrons in bloom near the village of Yumthang in North Sikkim

A J.D. Hooker drawing

FAMBONG LHO WILDLIFE SANCTUARY

Area: 51 square kilometres
Location: 20 kilometres away from Gangtok; Kangchendzonga visible from the north-west area.
Altitude: 1524 metres to 2749 metres.
Major species: Ferns, bamboo, wild orchids. rhododendron. Serow, Goral, Barking Deer, Himalayan Black Bear, Red Panda, Weasels, Martens, Leopard Cat, Marbled Cat, Civets and Binturong. Pheasants, eg the Satyr Tragopan, the Kalij Pheasant and Hill Partridges. Also varieties of Owl, Black Eagle, Green Pigeon, Slaty-headed Parakeet, Yellowbacked Sunbird, Collared Broadbill, Maroon Oriole, Bulbuls, Laughing Thrushes and Titmice.

has large snow white flowers, is another beautiful orchid common in Sikkim; at an altitude of 1,200 to 1,800 metres, it is found gracefully draped over rocks and tree stems. The *Arachanthe cathcartii*, a variety that prefers the moist warmth of the densely shaded tropical forests presents an amazing sight: thick fleshy flowers that grow to be more than 2 inches in diameter with curiously hinged lips and a colour scheme which make them look as if someone has painted chocolate stripes over their white bodies.

Commercial cultivation of orchids is becoming increasingly popular in Sikkim. It is usually done by individuals on a small scale and most of the produce

The queen of Himalayan flowers, the Blue poppy

is exported. The **Orchidarium** outside Gangtok, a sanctuary for several species of spectacular orchids, is worth a visit.

The tranquil **bamboo** groves of Sikkim are usually alive with birdsong. About thirty species of this tree-like grass belonging to the Bambusiae tribe are spread out over the tropical and temperate zones. The plant varies from short stems which form impenetrable thickets, to tall, elegantly fringed stalks that grow in shady groves. They vary in colour from the common greenish brown to the beautiful bluish shades of

Dendrobium nobile - one of Sikkim's most showy orchids flowers near the monastery of Tashiding in the spring

the *Arundinaria hookeriana* in the upper forests.

The role of bamboo in the lives of Sikkim's people cannot be over-estimated. The leaves provide good animal fodder and young shoots are cooked and eaten. The stems are used in constructing houses, building fences and as water conduits. The Lepchas are renowned for the suspension bridges they construct out of bamboo tied with reed. Bamboo and reed are also used to make baskets, machete sheathes, bows and arrows, tuks, mats and ornamental pins. Broad bamboo stems are the glasses in which chang, the Sikkimese drink, is sipped with the aid of slim bamboo straws.

WILDLIFE

Sikkim is strategically placed on the border area of two zoological zones: the Palearctic and the Oriental. As a result, fauna from two clearly demarcated groups coexist within its tiny area. This number and variety is further enriched by the occurrence of some animals from the Ethiopian zone.

Sikkim has its share of bugs, beetles and leeches, but in popular imagination it is the 'Valley of Butterflies'. Of the 1,400 **butterfly** species recorded in the Indian sub-continent, fifty per cent exist in Sikkim. What is more, since Sikkim is bound in by mountains on three sides, the butterfly population has been isolated, resulting in subspecies and forms that are quite distinct. For example, the *Lethe trisigmata* and the *Lethe atkinsoni* species have only been recorded in the Lachen and Lachung valleys of upper Sikkim. Some species like the common cabbage whites can be found right from the tropical area up to the alpine zone, but mostly each biotope is inhabited by a distinct set of species.

SHINGBA RHODODENDRON SANCTUARY

Area: 43 sq km
Location: In the Lachung Valley of North Sikkim. The road to Yumthang passes through the sanctuary.
Altitude: 2200 metres to 3500 metres
River: The Yumthang Chu
Major species: Rhododendron trees and shrubs, 40 species peculiar to Sikkim. Red Panda, Goral, Serow, Bharal, Himalayan Black Bear, weasels and two races of Musk Deer. Blood Pheasant, Monal Pheasant, Satyr Tragopan, Snow Partridge, Choughs, Finches and Blue Magpies.

KYONGNOSLA ALPINE SANCTUARY

Area: 4 sq km
Location: 31 km east of Gangtok on the way to Tsangu lake, extends from the 15th mile police check post upto and along the ridges bordering Rong Chu and Tsangu Lake.
Altitude: 3350 metres.
Major species: Rhododendrons, primulas, gentians and orchids between May and August. Rare and medicinal plants. Blood Pheasants and Monals, wrens, finches and warblers. Kestrels and Black Eagles; birds migrating between Siberia and India. Red Panda, Musk Deer, Serow, Goral, Leopard and Black Bear.

MAENAM WILDLIFE SANCTUARY

Area: 35 sq km
Location: Above the town of Rabongla in southern Sikkim. There is a beautiful one day trek through this forest to Maenam top and Bhaledunga.
Altitude: 2,100 metres to 3200 metres
Major species: The Blood Pheasant, Red Pandas, Civets, Black Eagles.

A Rose finch

However attempts are now being made to conserve and restore habitats. To this end, the Sikkim Nature Conservation Foundation has carried out a systematic survey of butterflies in the state and has published *Butterflies of Sikkim,* a useful and informative book.

Sikkim is said to contain more kinds of birds than any other area of comparable size the world over: its avian population extends to almost 600

A Himalayan green finch

The Rangit valley and the lower altitudes of the Tista valley that are between 900 metres and 1,800 metres, are the best areas to observe butterflies. Swallowtails abound here: emerald green Paris Peacocks glinting like gems as they bask in the sunlight; multi-hued Mormons flitting past in a shimmer of brilliant colour. Tigers, barons, pansies and sergeants are also common here. Beyond 1,800 metres, till almost 3,000 metres, the area is the domain of admirals, tortoiseshells, sliverstripes and silverspots. You might get lucky and catch a glimpse of the orange Queen of Spain Fritillary with its distinctive silver spots or the red and black Indian Red Admiral. Punches and Judies are also found in this area and the Striped Punch with its bright yellow wings broadly striped in black is a common sight. The colder heights beyond 3,000 metres are occupied by a few specialized species which have adapted to the harsh climactic conditions. The Mountain Tortoiseshell is peculiar to these high regions as is the Chumbi Green Underwing. Here, the low-flying Red Apollo with its semi-translucent white body marked heavily in black and red flits alongside the aggressive Great Satyr and the speckled Arctic Argus.

A sizable portion of Sikkim's butterfly habitat has been lost or endangered with deforestation and the indiscriminate use of pesticides.

known species. They vary in size from the gigantic Bearded Vulture which has a wingspan of 9.5 feet to the tiny red-breasted flowerpecker which could fit comfortably in a tea cup.

The richest bird life is found in the warm lower valleys. This is the habitat of many species of woodpeckers, most of the twenty-odd species of flycatchers for which Sikkim is renowned live in this area, the most spectacular of these being the male Paradise Flycatcher. The drongos also prefer the tropics as do the gregarious bulbuls, laughing thrushes, tits, babblers, four species of hornbills, and many of the state's birds of prey — falcons, eagles, hawks, vultures, kites, kestrels and owls.

The temperate zones are home to numerous species of cuckoos, robins, redstarts, sunbirds and mountain thrushes. Tubby brown Wood Snipe and Wood Cock probe the ground with their long rubbery bills. The Bearded Vulture lives high in the alpine zone and may

The state animal - the Red Panda

The snow leopard - one of the most endangered high altitude cats

be seen sailing in solitary, majestic splendour over mountain slopes, soaring to immense heights. This is finch country too, and most of Sikkim's 30 species live in this cold, rugged terrain. A variety of pheasants nest in these high altitudes including the Monal and the Blood Pheasant — Sikkim's official bird.

From warmth-loving, typically tropical animals to those who have made the snow-clad mountain peaks their home — Sikkim's mammal population covers the entire spectrum. In the tropical belt live varieties of mongoose, the sinuous martens and flying squirrels. Civet cats are common, the most striking being the Tiger Civet. Others felines that prefer these warmer foothills are the Marbled Cat and the Golden Cat. Amidst the thick foliage of the tall trees lives the unusual teddybear-like nocturnal creature called Binturong.

In the cooler woods beyond 1200 metres live yet more strange and beautiful animals. This is the territory

YETI !

Local people call it migyud and have always known of its existence: a gigantic creature six to nine feet in height, resembling a gorilla or an orangutang. They say it has uperhuman strength and is known to have napped the necks of yaks and other nimals. Even so, it was only when eminent nountaineers photographed inexplicable ootprints that the world began to take the possibility of the Yeti's actual existence seriously. In a world that thinks it has on its maps all the frontiers of knowledge, no amount of scientific exploration and research on the part of the western world has provided any further enlightenment on the reality of the Yeti. The mysterious beast continues to occupy a realm between legend and truth. Some Sikkimese believe that the Yeti is a spirit and hence cannot be seen. But zoologists are reluctant to dismiss the idea of this beast's existence. They hold that the still unexplored areas of Sikkim may well hold many ecological secrets, among them the Yeti. If Sikkimese monks are to be believed, the label Abominable Snowman does great injustice to the Yeti. They claim that the more pious and ascetic among them have friendly encounters, even exchanges with it. These monks meditating in isolated mountain caves leave offerings to the Yeti who, they say, brings them firewood in return.

of the elusive Clouded Leopard and the endearing State animal of Sikkim, the Red Panda. This member of the raccoon family is bright chestnut in colour with a vertical red stripe from eyes to neck. It has sharp pointed ears and a ringed tail, and usually moves around in families. The Muntjac or Barking Deer, the solitary Serow or Goat-antelope and the Goral antelope that also inhabit the temperate zones are beautiful, but are shy and therefore hard to spot. And up in the towering cliffs one may glimpse Himalayan Tahrs—reddish brown mountain goats with thick, unkempt coats.

The alpine regions is dominated by varieties of wild sheep, goat, oxen and antelope. Between the tree line and the snow line where there are pastures of rich grass, graze groups of Bharal or Blue Sheep, their slate blue coats blending perfectly with the blue shale and rock landscape. These unique creatures are an intermediate species between goat and sheep. Just within the tree line, on open ground, a variety of wild sheep—the Shapi—graze warily. Several species

of marmots live at these high altitudes as does the Orange Bellied Himalayan Squirrel and Musk Deer.

Well beyond the tree line may be found one of the highest-dwelling animals in the world, the Yak. This is a massively built member of the ox family, with a thick shaggy black coat. A male can weigh as much as 545 kilogrammes. Yaks live in large herds in the most desolate mountains where desert conditions prevail, feeding on moss, lichen, shrubs and melted snow. When their water source has frozen, they sustain themselves by eating ice. These animals have been domesticated and are prized as cattle. Strangely enough, domesticated yaks, unlike wild ones, often develop patches of white hair on their chest.

And up in the highest, most precipitous crags, a Snow Leopard may magically appear for an instant before disappearing again into the mists.

Human beings have predictably been the serpent in Sikkim's paradise. Once a world where man and nature lived in complete harmony, its

Banners in Gangtok to protest against the Rathong-Chu hydro electric project. Subsequently, the Government ceded to the wishes of the environmentalists and scrapped the project.

environment is now battling the destructive forces of modernity. Vast stretches of forests have fallen under the cement mixer, destroying entire hillsides, resulting in less rainfall, soil erosion, landslides and loss of habitat for animals and plants. There are the familiar problems of too many people with too many demands and too much pollution. Much of Sikkim's wonderful animal life is now on the brink of extinction. This includes not only the more spectacular larger birds and animals such as the Bearded Vulture, Black Eagle, Pheasants, the Snow Leopard (indiscriminately hunted for its beautiful coat), the Goral, Shapi and Serow, but many of the smaller animals too, like the Red Panda and the Clouded Leopard which have had their forest homes destroyed. In this grim battle of survival many of the creatures belonging to the warm forests of the lowlands have been forced to move to higher altitudes. The orchids and rhododendrons, the butterflies and bamboo: all are gasping for breath and space.

Recent government initiative is beginning to bear fruit, even if painfully slowly. Eco-resources have been identified and plans have been drawn up to prevent their exploitation and exhaustion. Trees have been planted, parks and sanctuaries created, while stringent laws attempt to curb hunting and tree-felling. The state now has a reasonably powerful environmentalist lobby which is trying to monitor projects like dam constructions to ensure that these are done within a framework of eco-friendly guidelines. However, for many fragile species of plant and animal life, this concern may prove fatally belated.

Sikkim's extremely fragile eco-system needs help from its citizens and tourists if it is to survive.

A Naturalist in the Himalaya

The first attempt to systematically explore the land and to document information about the flora and fauna of the Eastern Himalaya was done by the British botanist Joseph Dalton Hooker—son of William Jackson Hooker, the first Director of Kew Gardens. In fact, father and son were virtually synonymous with British botany for all of the nineteenth century. The younger Hooker obtained his MD from University of Glasgow in 1839 and then travelled extensively for most of his life on botanical expeditions (including one to the Antarctic region), publishing prolifically on his findings and theories. He was a close friend of Darwin's and was a pioneering scientist in the application of evolutionary theory to botany. In 1848 he came to Sikkim to study the vegetation of temperate and tropical regions. His year-long travels resulted in an amazing documentation of the numerous species of animal and plant life, many of which turned out to be completely new biological and botanical discoveries. Many species of orchids, rhododendrons and ferns are named after Hooker in acknowledgement of his having brought them to the notice of the western world. He published the *Rhododendrons of Sikkim* in 1849; while Hooker's *Himalayan Journals*—a record of his travels in Sikkim and surrounding regions —is a classic, valued by naturalists and even historians and sociologists. The stunning botanical drawings in the book are now valued as works of art. Hooker succeeded his father to the Directorship of Kew in 1865 and he died in 1911.

"… the sun, the moon, and the stars, trees and plants, animals, birds and insects, act as our infallible calendars, time keepers…and guides…our very existence is inextricably bound up and interwoven with these things that God has given us."

Lepcha, My Vanishing Tribe by A.R. Foning

Sikkim's people are almost entirely composed of three groups: the Lepchas, the Bhutias and the Nepalese. Of these, the Nepalese, themselves a conglomeration of diverse ethnic types, make up the largest number. Besides these three groups, there are a small number of plainsmen from other parts of India, especially Biharis and Marwaris, as well as refugees fleeing Chinese-occupied Tibet and Drukpas from Bhutan. Despite this diversity, a remarkable level of tolerance makes the Sikkimese a harmonious community. Over the years there has been cultural cross-pollination, especially between the Lepchas and the Bhutias, leading to the evolution of a distinctive Sikkimese ethos. Evidence of this acculturation is the absorption of components of the Lepcha religion into Buddhist ritual.

The Lepchas, who call themselves

Nepali women at the Gayzing haat

The People of Sikkim

the Rong-pa, were Sikkim's earliest inhabitants. For the Lepchas, the entire natural world is imbued with living spirits: every rock, every tree, mountain, river and animal is endowed with a spirit, sometimes good and sometimes evil. And each of these supernatural creatures have their own set of legends. Serpents dam rivers, dead infants are reborn as pine trees and humans fly over mountains. The presiding deity for the Lepchas is Mount Kangchendzonga, who is loved as protector but feared for

his wrath. Mount Tendong, on the other hand, is supposed to have saved many lives during a great flood, and so is worshipped with gratitude. And among the high peaks, hidden from sight by Kangchendzonga and impossible to reach, is the valley of Mayel, the land of the Lepcha forefathers who enjoy the secret of eternal life.

Most rivers and mountains have Lepcha names and nearly all play a prominent part in Lepcha folklore. The people have an amazing, intimate knowledge of their environment. They are able to identify at a glance the species of each genus of plants, every animal, bird and insect. Their language, dubbed a mystery language since philologists have not been able to agree on its origins, has a well-stocked vocabulary for a variety of flora, fauna and natural phenomena. The Lepchas converted to Buddhism in the seventeenth century and later, with the arrival of the missionaries, some became Christians, but a strong strain of their primitive worship persists even today. Their songs, dances and folklore stress their inextricable link with the natural world.

Government has reserved the Dzongu area for the Lepchas. This is a heavily forested region bordered in the north by the peaks of the Kangchendzonga range. Till recently, the Lepchas in this area were protected from modern influences, their only contact with the outside world being the market place of Mangan where they come to barter or sell the orange and cardamom crops they grew. Their villages were largely inaccessible,

Previous page: A Lepcha boy near the village of Singhik

having to be reached by narrow paths through steep ravines. Today these bridle paths have been widened to make motorable roads. Cane and bamboo bridges have given way to steel constructions. Hospitals and schools have been opened in the remotest villages. Nepalis and plainsmen have invaded the sanctuary taking advantage of the rapidly dwindling Lepcha population. The beauty and wisdom of ancient Lepcha tradition and culture will have to fight to survive modernity.

The Bhutias are mainly descendants of the early settlers from Tibet and Bhutan who accompanied the ancestors of the first Chogyal when he went to Sikkim in the sixteenth century. Members of the former Namgyal dynasty belonged to this ethnic group. Earlier Bhutias had three distinct social classes: the aristocracy, the landholders and administrators and the commoners. With the dissolution of the institution of the Chogyal, such social distinctions have ceased to have relevance.

Mother and son at Muguthang village

The Bhutias are mainly farmers: the pastures of the North are used by them to graze the yaks and cattle that they

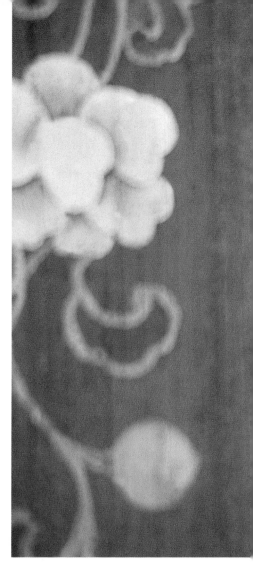

breed. The apples from their orchards find markets even outside Sikkim. Their population is spread out in pockets throughout the state. However, they are concentrated in the North where the Bhutias live in villages administered by elected phipons or village headmen.

Bhutias retain strong links with their Tibetan origins and until recently, when the Tibet border was sealed off by the Chinese, Bhutias would regularly visit Tibet both to trade and to keep in touch with their families. Tibetan Buddhism permeates Bhutia life. Nearly every Bhutia family has one male member who has entered the lamasery to become a monk and until recently, with education coming under the

exclusive purview of the monasteries, monks were the intellectual elite of Bhutia society. Today, however, education has become far more widespread; white-collar jobs and government posts are now considered equally indicative of social mobility. Monasteries are still the focal points of festivals, ceremonies and other social events. Even the art of contemporary Bhutias—their woven mats and blankets, their intricately carved boxes, their exquisite thankhas—derives, as did the art of their ancestors, from Buddhist spirituality.

The greatest influx of Nepalese people into Sikkim took place around the eighteenth century with the active encouragement of the British, but oral records of the Limbu and Rai tribes suggest that Nepalese had begun migrating to Sikkim from the poorer eastern regions of Nepal much earlier.

Now Sikkim's largest community, they are made up of several ethnic groups, like the Magars, Murmis, Newars, Tamangs, Sherpas, Gurungs, Rais, Limbus, Damais, Kamis, Bahuns (Brahmins) and the Chettris. The Newars, who are renowned as craftsmen, are said to have fashioned the earliest coinage of Sikkim in the nineteenth century, operating the first mints in the country. Some of these groups have their distinct language, but as a general rule Nepalese is understood

Watching the Pang Lhabsol festivities at Tsuklakhang, Gangtok

Unloading a Sikkim Nationalised Transport (SNT) bus at Gangtok. The SNT services remain the lifeline for the people between the villages and the capital Gangtok.

by all and forms the lingua franca. Both the Buddhism and the Hinduism that most Nepalese practice are tempered by the strong presence of elements of tribal worship patterns making their culture as unique and colourful as that of the Lepchas and the Bhutias.

The earliest Nepalese settlers were share-croppers who introduced the concept of terrace farming into Sikkimese agriculture. Even now, the majority of Nepalese are farmers and the population is concentrated in the lower valleys of the East, West and South. However, they are undoubtedly the most socially mobile community in Sikkim. Most important government posts and professional jobs are held by

Sikkimese women in matching bakus walk along a Gangtok street

Sikkimese elders pray at the Queen Mother's funeral at Gangtok

them. Their drive and diverse skills have made them power the modernization of Sikkim. They are also renowned for their martial skills and large numbers of Nepalese from Sikkim serve as soldiers in both the British and Indian armies in Gurkha regiments.

About seventy per cent of Sikkim's people live in villages, mostly in the valleys created by the Tista and Rangit rivers. The Eastern region, which includes Gangtok, has the highest population while Northern Sikkim, with its inhospitable terrain and harsh climate, is very sparsely populated. The early settlement pattern of the ethnic groups followed, by and large, their economic interests; the Bhutias preferring the higher alpine pastures for their cattle, the Lepchas the forests of the middle valleys and the Nepalese the lower valleys for their farming. Today,

Lamas watch the masked dances at Rumtek monastery

however, mobility propelled by economic ambitions has rearranged these patterns, leading to more even ethnic distribution in certain areas.

Much of the rural area has electricity, and almost all villages are connected by motorable roads and a postal service. Government healthcare clinics have been established in far-flung areas and educational institutions providing free tuition right uptil the university level are wide-spread. Most Sikkimese are fluent in Nepalese and the educated are conversant in English. The most widely-used script is Devanagri.

Despite the changes that have occurred as a corollary to modernization, traditional Sikkimese culture endures in everyday life and is most evident in the villages, which make them rewarding places to visit. In the countryside, you can still see people in their richly colourful traditional garb that is distinctive for each community. Elsewhere, the logic of modernization is swallowing up difference. Urban centres, especially the capital Gangtok, have all the trappings of contemporary living: departmental stores, fast-food parlours and hip youth in Reeboks and Levis, sometimes made in America, but more usually in Gangtok's back alleys. Businessmen, government officials and executives sport three-piece suits that could be seen anywhere in the world. It is only the old who can sometimes be seen in Sikkimese clothes. Similarly, traditional outdoor sports, which included archery and hunting, have given way to soccer, fast becoming a national pastime. Paljor Stadium in Gangtok is the venue of a major tournament, the Governor's Gold Cup. Communal singing, verse-competitions and dancing were the way the people of Sikkim entertained themselves in earlier times, but today there are cinema halls even in remote villages and the

Hindi film industry dominates here as it does elsewhere in India. However, some ancient board games, like Sho and Ba, mostly gambling games, have survived.

THE LEGEND OF LEGSHIP

A group of people were once passing through Legship in western Sikkim. They saw a smooth stone formed in the shape of the Shiva Linga that is worshipped by the Hindus. One man became curious and tried to lift it, but it was so heavy that he could not even move it. Others tried but the small stone proved impossible to budge. The news of this mysterious stone spread far and wide and at last reached the learned lamas of Pemayangtse monastery. The lamas understood that the stone must be a sacred object with heavenly powers and felt that it should be kept in a proper place of worship. So somehow they managed to lift it and carried it to their own monastery. Here they kept it under lock and key in the sanctuary.
That night a tremendous storm broke out. The wind howled and rain lashed against the walls of the monastery and threatened to blow it down. Lightning lit up the eerie hills. The next morning when they unlocked the sanctuary, the stone had vanished! The lamas concluded that the stone must have somehow returned to Legship, and sure enough when they went to Legship the stone was standing in its original place. The lamas realized that the stone wanted to be left here, so after worshipping it with respect they returned to their monastery. The stone began to attract many people who came to worship the Linga. A temple was built to enshrine it, and the temple of Legship is today a famous Shiva temple.

Lamas lead the funeral procession of the Queen Mother of Sikkim from the Gangtok Palace to the cremation grounds at Lukshyama hill

FORTY- NINE DAY CEREMONY OF THE BUDDHISTS

The Buddhist death ceremony is most elaborate. The corpse is not disturbed until a qualified lama has extracted the soul in the orthodox way: otherwise the soul might get brutally ejected, lose its way, and get seized by a demon. Thus, immediately after death, a white cloth is thrown over the face of the corpse and the pho-o lama is sent for. The lama sits with the corpse and chants a service which contains directions for the soul to reach the Western Paradise. The lama plucks a few strands of hair from the corpse's head, to signify the freeing of the spirit. More directions are then given to the spirit about the dangers on the way to Paradise—the demons it might meet and how to conduct itself safely. Relatives and guests are then invited and a period of feasting begins, while the lamas continue to advise and guide the spirit with their chants. The corpse is offered fresh food and drink everyday. Within a few days, sometimes hours, of death, the corpse is taken for burial or cremation after being offered a special feast. The ceremonies continue till forty-nine days after death. An effigy of the deceased is made by dressing a block of wood in the deceased's clothes. Food and drink is placed before this effigy just as was done with the corpse and the lamas continue with their chanting and offerings. During this time, the death demons are also exorcised from the house. Finally, on the forty-ninth day, the death service is concluded with ceremonial burning of the face of the effigy.

Lhonak,
The Home of the Herdsmen

"....here the colourings are those of the fiery desert.... while the
climate is that of the poles. Never, in the course of all my wanderings,
had my eye rested on a scene so dreary and inhospitable.
Himalayan Journals by Sir Joseph Dalton Hooker

*The village of
Muguthang,
home of the
herdsmen of
Lhonak*

*Previous page:
A yak caravan
crosses the
North Sikkim
plateau
between
Donkung and
Cholamu in the
rain shadow of
the Himalaya*

The climb to the top of the pass seemed to go on forever. We had completed
the ascent to the top of the first ridge: there were two more ridges to cross
before reaching the pass. My friend Naresh, a young doctor with the Indian
Army based at Thangu in North Sikkim, seemed to be climbing much more
easily —perhaps his long stay at high altitudes had ensured acclimatization.

It was a cold and damp May morning with clouds rushing up the valley
and most of the surrounding hills white with snow. We plodded through the
soft snow sinking knee deep, sometimes waist deep in places. The going was
slow and breathing became more difficult as we climbed higher. Suddenly,
the gradient eased and we found the cairns at the top. We had reached the top
of Lhonak La (5,300 metres) which guards the entrance to the remote Lhonak
valley in North Sikkim. The valleys to the east were far below us, while to the
west, the pass dropped in a steep snow-clad slope to the bottom. Most of the
surrounding peaks were covered with dark ominous clouds and snow began
to fall as we started our descent.

Lhonak, meaning 'barren plain', is Sikkim's mystery valley. The Lhonak La
pass provides the only accessible link to the rest of the state. To the south of
Lhonak lie the impregnable Himalaya, while the Tibetan border to the north

and the peaks of Nepal to the west create an isolated pocket in the rain shadow of Kangchendzonga. There are other passes in Sikkim which are higher and steeper than the Lhonak La, but none more hazardous. Snow-bound for more than nine months in the year, and frequently fed by icy winds from Tibet, it is the scene of numerous snow storms and blizzards. Lhonak remains for most of the year a broad flat featureless plain—cold, grey and windy. A near magical three-month break occurs in summer when primulas, dwarf rhododendrons and many other Himalayan flowers burst into bloom transforming the valley. This brief interlude ends as suddenly as it had begun and browns and greys return to dominate a severe landscape. The peaks are rocky and harsh and the winds blow for most of the day and night : sometimes gently and sometimes with vicious intensity.

About a hundred herdsmen have their homes built of stone adjacent to the Naku Chu river at Muguthang (4,400 metres), the principal village of the valley, about an hour and a half's walk from the foot of the Lhonak La. Natives of the village of Khampa Dzong in Tibet, these herdsmen had fled from Tibet during the Chinese aggression in 1959 and settled in this valley. Their nomadic lifestyle, grazing yaks, sheep and goats, takes them to different parts of Lhonak during the year, depending on the availability of pasture land and water. The twelve stone houses of Muguthang are their permanent homes though they use tents made of yak wool as temporary shelters while travelling from place to place. Prior to the Chinese aggression, the Tibetans of Khampa Dzong used to migrate to the Lhonak valley in summer to graze their cattle and return to Tibet in the winter. Now with bayonets and gunfire across the passes, Lhonak—a barren wilderness that is a mere extension of the Tibetan plateau—is their home.

Unlike other shepherds in the Himalaya who migrate to the high altitude pastures in summer and return to the valleys in winter, the herdsmen in Lhonak

Tending a fire at a Muguthang home

Lama La teaches at the Muguthang school

do neither. They merely move during winter to areas that are even bleaker, windswept and naturally free of snow. West of the village of Muguthang are the grazing grounds of Tongpen, Janak and Thuktsop which receive the direct impact of the winds from Tibet. Despite the sub zero temperatures, snow rarely lies heavy on the ground and man and animal manage to survive the harsh winter.

The inaccessibility of the Lhonak La pass in winter makes it necessary to stock up on supplies during summer. When the pass is relatively free of snow in July-August, yak caravans leave Muguthang for Lachen—the roadhead at an altitude of 2,700 metres and a two-day walk down the Tista valley. From Lachen, a ride in a lorry or the weekly bus takes the herdsmen to the capital Gangtok where food and other supplies are readily available. Returning to Lachen, the yaks are loaded up with provisions and the caravan begins it's journey back to Muguthang.

On our arrival at Muguthang, we met Lama Tsewang who is known in the valley as Lama La. Lama La is the schoolmaster of the Muguthang Lower Primary School set up by the Sikkim Government in 1980. Educated at the Central Institute of Tibetan Higher Studies in far away Banaras, in the sun baked plains of Gangetic India, Lama La has a Bachelor of Arts degree in Buddhist philosophy and speaks fluent English. What is he doing in Muguthang divorced from the mainstream of Sikkimese life?

"My home and my family are here," he declares, "ever since we left Tibet, Lhonak has been our home. My brothers graze yak and sheep all over the valley, I must be here to help them." he adds simply.

Lama La often takes classes in his courtyard outside the house as it is warmer outdoors during summer. The school, with nineteen students, has education facilities upto Class 3 after which students must go to school at Lachen and later to the district headquarters at Mangan.

The next day Lama La invited us to visit his cousins at the neighbouring village of Naku about a three-hour walk from Muguthang, and adjacent to the border with Tibet. "They are grazing our cattle as good pastureland is available," he explained and suggested that we use riding yaks for our visit.

The morning dawned fine and the north-east flank of Kangchendzonga was visible to the south as we reached Lama La's house. The yaks were ready and saddled and Lama La held the reins as I heaved myself astride one of them. Within a few seconds, I had been thrown clear of the yak and landed on the ground with a resounding thud! The yak bolted across the Naku Chu river with Lama La in hot pursuit. Eventually after a strenuous chase, the yak was caught and brought back. However the beast steadfastly refused to cooperate and we had to decide to walk upto Naku.

At Naku, we found Lama La's cousins Norbu and his wife making tea inside their yak wool tent. The interior of the tent was beautifully decorated with homespun woollen blankets and cushions of exquisite designs and colours. We sat down near the yak-dung fire for a welcome cup of tea and Lama La told us about their life on the barren plateau.

" The yak is our lifeline with survival," he declared, "it provides us with food, clothing and shelter."

The local yak cheese known as churpi, yak butter, and yak milk are all used by the family and dried yak meat is a delicacy for festive occasions. The yak wool is used in the making of tents and the weaving of blankets and rugs to be sold at Gangtok. Sometimes, the herdsmen tide over difficult times by selling yaks, which may fetch as much as Rs 5,000 per yak. However, attacks by predators cannot be ruled out and herdsmen have been known to lose as many as twenty sheep in a year to snow leopards and other high altitude cats. Some years ago a liverfluke infestation killed a large number of cattle in Lhonak. As many as 300 yaks and about 800 sheep were killed by this epidemic and peculiarly all chose the same place to die. Christened the 'yak graveyard' by Lama La, this part of the valley is strewn with skeletons and bones of the dead animals.

Lama La told us about the Drukpa Tsechi festival. Celebrated on the fourth day of the sixth month of the Tibetan Buddhist lunar calendar, prayers

A Muguthang family at home

are held and offerings made to Lord Buddha by the villagers of Lhonak. The piece de resistance of the festival is the grand yak race on the broad maidan near Muguthang with both the yaks and their riders dressed in their ceremonial finery and egged on by the enthralled crowds.

It was late afternoon as Norbu left the tent to round up the yaks for the night. We decided to leave as we had to return to Muguthang by sunset. Lama La spoke of the problems of his tribe as we walked through the bleak plateau. "Despite all our efforts to promote education, a large number of children refuse to come to school— they prefer to accompany their parents with the yak herds across the valley," he said sadly. Lama La feels that the difficulty in communication is responsible for the relative isolation of the Lhonak valley and as a result there is very little contact with the outside world.

"An unique lifestyle," mused Lama La, "and far removed from the material world of today."

We watched Norbu vanish over the hill to round up his cattle, and my mind flashed back to the herdsmen in other parts of Sikkim: at Cholamu near the source of the river Tista, at Donkung below the snowy dome of Mount Kanchenjao, at Dzongri in the shadow of Mount Pandim, herdsmen like Norbu were out on the pastures, accompanied by their Tibetan mastiffs, shepherding their cattle to safer ground.

The muted tinkling of yak bells could be heard as we neared Muguthang. It was dusk and fires were being lit in the houses. Huddled in my down jacket to ward off the cold, I watched from a promontory the glimmering shapes of yaks returning to the village with their owners. They passed by, oblivious to their harsh surroundings. Man and nature seemed to be inextricably interwoven until they almost seemed to be one on that broad immense landscape in the rain shadow of the Himalayas.

The yak graveyard in the Lhonak valley

Overleaf: Sheep leave for pasture in the early morning from Muguthang village

"A purer air surrounds it, a white clarity envelopes it and the Gods there taste of a happiness which lasts as long as their eternal lives."

Homer

Previous page: At Lachung monastery

Dancers at the monastery of Rumtek during the annual chaam dances. Rumtek is the premier monastery of the Kargyupa sect of Buddhism.

BUDDHISM

In the seventeenth century three wise men from Tibet travelled to Sikkim and marked the arrival of a new epoch in the land's history. For they were the harbingers of Buddhism, which was to establish itself as the single most influential factor in the social, political and cultural development of the land. Hinduism and Buddhism dominate the spiritual landscape of Sikkim— Hinduism by its numbers and Buddhism by the extent of its cultural influence.

Sikkim received the teachings of the Buddha in the form that these had been transmuted by Tibetan culture and Sikkim, in turn, exerted its own influence on Tibetan Buddhism so that the Buddhism practised in Sikkim came to possess a distinct character. Today, Buddhism modulates and moulds the lives of its followers: monasteries are still the centre of village life and the most striking architectural features in the Sikkim landscape; Buddhist rites and customs are faithfully followed; lamas command respect and reverence and are crucial for any ceremony; Buddhist festivals dominate the Sikkim calendar and the Buddhist calendar dictates the rhythm of daily life for the majority of the people.

The earliest schism in Buddhism resulted in the **Hinayana** and **Mahayana** traditions. Hinayana survives in Sri Lanka, Burma and Thailand and is the more conservative school. The Mahayana sect emerged from contact with Hinduism and had far greater popular appeal since the abstruse metaphysics of Hinayana were here greatly modified. Mahayana is the pan-Asiatic form of Buddhism and spread from India to Central Asia, China, Japan, Java and Sumatra. Among the many smaller sub-schools of Buddhism that developed as the religion spread over a vast area, one which developed in India was the Tantra movement which was heavily influenced by gnostic and magical currents prevalent at the time and whose central aim was the swift achievement of liberation.

TIBETAN BUDDHISM OR LAMAISM

The distinctive form of Buddhism that developed in Tibet is a synthesis of Mahayana Buddhism with Tantrism. Tibetan Buddhism also adopted, in a modified form, many practices from the pre-existing shamanistic Bon cult such as oracular priests, local divinities, charms and spells. Buddhism first gained recognition in Tibet during the reign of Srong-brtsan-sgampo (620-649), two of whose wives were devout Buddhists and encouraged him to convert. One wife came to be later regarded in popular tradition as the incarnation of the Buddhist saviour Dolma. The religion received active encouragement during the reign of Khri-Srong-Ide-btsan (775-797) when the first monastery was built at Samye, the first seven monks or lamas were ordained and the celebrated Tantrik master Padmasambhava was invited to visit.

During the tenth and eleventh century, noblemen in western Tibet encouraged learned Tibetans to travel to India in quest of books and masters and to translate sacred texts. With the visit of the Indian master Atisa Dipankara from India in 1042, Buddhism was firmly established as the dominant religion in Tibet, and under Atisa the importance of monastic discipline received great emphasis. The various lamaic sects date back to his visit. He founded the highly ascetic **Kadamapa** sect; those unreformed by Atisa became the **Nyingmapa** or old sect. In the latter half of the eleventh century a third sect, the **Kargyupa**, was established by the saint Makpa. The Kadamapa sect, more than three centuries later, would become the more modified **Gelukpa** sect—founded in the fourteenth century by the learned Tshongkhapa who wanted to reform the laxity he perceived in the moral fibre of

The Ceremonial Dances: Pang Lhabsol & Kagyet

was a very wet September in Gangtok. The incessant rains had breached the Tista valley road in a number of places disrupting communications between the Sikkimese capital and the plains of Bengal. The Border Roads Organisation were hard at work trying to clear the landslide debris but it was not an easy task.

I was on my way to Gangtok to photograph the Pang Lhabsol dances. The journey took the whole day instead of the customary five hours because of the bad roads and I reached Gangtok in the evening amidst pouring rain. At Hotel Tibet that night, I

The Pang Lhabsol procession circles the Tsuklakhang during the annual festival at the Gangtok palace

the monks. Today the Gelukpa is the dominant sect in Tibet.

With the growth of different sects, and the increase in the temporal power of monasteries, rivalry between the various sects became intense and different sects allied themselves with different political powers. In the seventeenth century, the head of the Gelukpa sect—known traditionally as the Dalai Lama—appealed to a Mongol chieftain for help against the Karmapa sect whose patrons were the rulers of Gtsang. After the defeat of Gtsang forces, the Mongols gifted Tibet to the Dalai Lama as a religious offering, and from 1642 until its occupation by the Chinese in the 1950s, the Gelukpas were the dominant sect in Tibet with the Dalai Lama its temporal and spiritual head. The Gelukpas are commonly known as the Yellow Hats because of their costume.

Lamas and villagers erect a new prayer flag at Pemayangtse monastery on Sikkimese New Years day

The warrior dance at the Tsuklakhang monastery

bumped into Tseten Baro the Manager. The dances were likely to be washed out as the rains showed no signs of abating, I remarked sadly.

"It will stop raining during the dances," Tseten announced like a veritable soothsayer.

"How do you know that?" I asked.

"The lamas are praying in the Palace—the rains must stop," he proclaimed.

I shook my head in rationalist disbelief and went to bed.

The most important of all the ceremonial dances in Sikkim is the Pang Lhabsol or the worship of the snowy ranges, dedicated to the presiding deity Kangchendzonga. It was started by Chador Namgyal, the third Chogyal and is performed on the fifteenth day of the seventh month of the Tibetan lunar calendar corresponding to around August or September. To prepare for the dances, the lamas retreat to the west cave of Dechenphu situated near the yak pastureland of Dzongri. In Gangtok, the dances are performed in the Tsuklakhang, the royal chapel, adjacent to the Palace.

The next day I was at Tsuklakhang at the appointed hour. Amazingly, the rain had stopped and rays of sunshine were trying to

Wangchuk Namgyal watches the Pang Lhabsol dances at Suklakhang monastery in Gangtok

silk sashes worn crosswise used to be worn even by the ancient warriors in battles. The god Kangchendzonga is represented in a red mask, mounted on a white snow lion. He is invoked as the war god in Sikkim. The climax of the dance is the appearance of Mahakala, the guardian spirit of the faith who asks Kangchendzonga to save the religion and to bring peace and prosperity amongst the Sikkimese people. The dances begin when the Chogyal and the Royal family arrive from the Palace and seat themselves in the pavilion opposite the monastery. The ceremonies end with the handing of water and flour to the dancers who make the offerings to the gods.

filter through the clouds. The prayers of the lamas had been answered.

The Warrior dance is the highlight of the Pang Lhabsol festivities. The dancers are dressed as warriors in helmets with swords and shields. The

Situated across the valley from the capital Gangtok, Rumtek has become the most famous monastery in Sikkim. Film-maker Ramesh

The head lama at Phodang monastery during the Kagyet dances

Yellow hat lamas preside over the dances at Rumtek monastery

ama watches the masked dances at Enchey monastery in Gangtok

According to legend Guru Padmasambhava (or Guru Rimpoche as he is known in Sikkim) visited Sikkim in the eighth century and consecrated the religious spots of Sikkim. However, it was not until the seventeenth century that Buddhism made its first real impact on Sikkim society. At this time three lamas belonging to various sub-sects of the Nyingmapa sect entered Sikkim from different directions and convened at Yoksam. The chief of these was Lhatsun Chenpo. Here they crowned Phuntsog Namgyal the first Chogyal of Sikkim. And while the Chogyal undertook the political consolidation of Sikkim, the lamas went about building monasteries and shrines for the propagation of the Buddhist Dharma. Sikkimese Buddhism combines Tibetan Buddhism with elements of the aboriginal Lepcha religion, the most striking example of this being the incorporation of the worship of Kangchendzonga into Sikkimese Buddhism.

There are now two lamaic sects in Sikkim: the Nyingmapa and the Kargyupa. The **Nyingmapa** is the primitive, "unreformed" sect of Tibetan Buddhism, imbued with pre-Buddhist religious practices. The monks, distinctive in their red hats, seldom practise celibacy or abstinence. Sikkim's renowned Pemayangtse monastery belongs to the Nyingmapa sect, the only one that worships Guru Rimpoche (or Padmasambhava) as the second Buddha.

The guardian deity of the **Kargyupa** sect is the Lord of the Black Cloak. The head of the Kargyupa sect is known as the Karmapa. Traditionally, the seat of the Kargyupa is in Tsurphu, Tibet. However, with the Chinese occupation of Tibet the sixteenth Karmapa was forced to flee the country with many of his followers. They were invited to settle in Sikkim by Chogyal Tashi Namgyal and their centre became the Rumtek Monastery. Along with the Karmapa came the four high tulkus, priests of the Kargyu order. After the death of the sixteenth Karmapa in 1982, the onus of carrying the cumulative wisdom of this ancient sect lies with the tulkus until the seventeenth incarnation is found.

Sharma made a film on Rumtek which won him an award and sent him on the road to success. The film star Kabir Bedi's mother was said to have meditated in Rumtek. The monastery belonging to the Kargyu-pa sect of Buddhism was set up by the Gwalya Karmapa after he fled from Tibet during the Chinese aggression in 1962. Unlike the other Sikkimese monasteries, the construction is very Tibetan in character.

The Rumtek 'chaams' or ceremonial dances are held in winter each year. The Rumtek lamas wore yellow hats which contrasted strikingly with their maroon robes and the entire ritual was simultaneously impressive as well as terrifying. The Rumtek lamas were not camera shy—in fact, the large influx of foreigners to Rumtek makes this one of the most frequented monasteries in Sikkim.

The other great event in Sikkim are th Kagyet dances at Phodang monastery. The danc are celebrated on the twenty-eighth and twent ninth day of the tenth month of the Tibet. lunar calendar, during Sikkimese New Year. It as spectacular to watch as the Pang Lhabsol.

Situated on the North Sikkim highway whi snakes it's way above the precipitous gorge the river Tista, Phodang is one and a half hou drive from Gangtok. The drive to Phodang winter is punctuated with scintillating views Kangchendzonga soaring above the clouds a the scarlet flash of poinsettia blossoms at the ed, of the forest. The monastery stands on a sp above the highway and is one of the largest Sikkim. The original monastery has been rebu and the new building has a large number of mu paintings depicting various stages in the life Buddha.

Buddhists believe individuals to be incarnations or reborn forms of persons who lived in the past. Saintly men are often found to be incarnations of saints who may have lived centuries earlier. Tests, signs on the body and behaviour patterns reveal whether a person is an incarnation or not. In the case of the head of sects, such as the Dalai Lama or the Karmapa, they are continuously reborn to carry on with the work of saving earthly creatures. It is said that the sixteenth Karmapa, at the time of his death, left behind a prediction letter with detailed instructions about his next birth. The boy who is discovered to be the seventeenth Karmapa will be put through a series of tests before he is acknowledged as the incarnate. After his discovery and enthronement he will undergo a rigorous training starting with the basic Buddhist tenets. He will then gradually be initiated into the meditative techniques peculiar to the Kargyupa sect. Only when a child meets all the criterion is he accepted and enthroned.

The Kalachakra Tantra

This is regarded as one of the most profound teachings of the Buddha. It is recorded in Buddhist history as the 12,000-stanza long Kalachakra Mul-tantra and is said to have been taught by the Buddha in the form of the deity Kalachakra at Shambala in Central Asia. The Kalachakra was introduced into Tibet in the eleventh century and the cosmology and astrology of Tibetan Buddhism derives from this tantra. One important feature of Kalachakra is that it encourages mass initiation. The Dalai Lama is traditionally, a qualified teacher of the Kalachakra and the present Dalai Lama performed the initiation at the Kalachakra Initiation ceremony which was held in Sikkim in 1993.

tense moment during the Kagyet dances at Phodang

A masked dancer performs at Rumtek

The Kagyet dances are usually held in December and on my first visit, it was one of the oldest 'Kagyets' that one could imagine.

From early morning, Sikkimese from near and far begin to gather at the monastery. Most of them come from the nearby villages, some from Gangtok and others from Mangan, the district headquarters of North Sikkim. Numerous shops

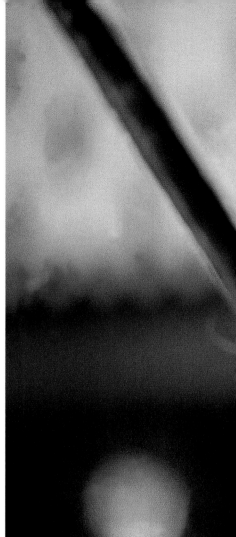

A Skeleton dancer at the Phodang chaams

sprout overnight selling Lepcha medicinal herbs, trinkets, hot momos and chhang and the usual assortment of Indian 'delicacies' that one could expect to see at a country fair. I remember particular fascinating sweet shop selling ladoos and other esoterica of the most bizarre colours and sizes which were gulped down by the local children with gay abandon.

Prior to the dances, prayers are offered by the lamas inside the main chapel of the monastery. During the festival, eleven dances are performed in the large courtyard. Most of these dances deal with the victory of good over evil. The dances begin with the band playing a peculiar dirge-like medley of sound. To the newcomer, the sound at first may seem out of tune, but, as the ears become accustomed to the din, a definite rhythm

becomes discernable and the music begins to ta[ke] shape in the mind. The bass notes of the gre[at] horn or 'Bardo Lamsol' seem to boom with th[e] message of the gods, the thunder and lightni[ng] over the high passes, the roar of the migh[ty] avalanches on the highest peaks. The mus[ic] signifies the limitlessness of time and space [in] the heart of the mystic Himalaya where man [is] reincarnated through eternity.

The dances carry on throughout the day. Th[e] monks wear long silken robes, beautiful[ly] embroidered, while on their heads are som[e] outrageous masks. Intended to represent differe[nt] animals and birds such as yaks, deer, goats, shee[p,] horses, eagles, they ridicule nature. The Skelet[on] Dance is particularly terrifying with four dance[rs] enacting a scene of death. They wear 'skull' mas[ks]

A clown at the Phodang Kagyet dances

d are dressed in white brocade. Initially, the
sic sounds like a dirge and the dancers move
wly. As the music rises to a frenzy, they pirouette
th amazing speed, their legs kicked high in time
th the banging of drums and the clashing of
mbals. Almost as abruptly as it begins, the dance
ds and the dancers retreat inside the monastery
landed with white 'khadas' or ceremonial
rves for a particularly outstanding performance.
The festival culminates with the performance
the 'Black Hat' which signifies a victory for
ddhism and is watched with bated breath by
enthralled crowds.
As it ended, dusk drew near, and a threatening
k of grey black clouds covered the sky. The
lagers began to leave the monastery with
ewell chants of 'Om Mani Padme Hum'. The

lamas armed with their cymbals, trumpets and
prayer books assembled before the entrance of
the monastery to enact the final ritual. I was one
of the last visitors left standing on the monastery
steps as I photographed them in the fading light..
Their chanting carried on oblivious to the icy
winds and the nagging rain. Another 'Kagyet' was
over and Sikkim looked forward to the prosperity
of the coming year.

THE LAMAS

Lamas are the Buddhist priests. Traditionally, the second son of every Bhutia family would become a lama. Now most monasteries accept boys from non-Bhutia families too. Further, while the monks of Pemayangtse are required to be celibate, few other lamas are expected to follow the rule of celibacy.

The little aspiring monk is brought to the monastery usually between the ages of eight and ten. He is given a thorough physical examination. If he passes this, he is handed over to the tutelage of a senior lama and enters a period of probation. At this stage he is like any other school boy, though his hair is cropped and he lives at the monastery. This lasts for about three years, and if he proves himself to be fairly intelligent he becomes a novitiate. Now he must abide by monastic rules; he must shave his head, take his vows, dress in lama robes and take on a religious name. His confirmation ceremony is an elaborate affair that has to be financed by his family. And then he begins a series of examinations all of which he must pass before he can be free of menial duties. He has to learn the many scriptural books by heart and train in all the rites and ceremonies of Buddhist worship. He can visit his home, but must return within a stipulated time. As he passes his examinations he is gradually promoted until he is qualified enough to be received within the Order. And with each graduation, his duties become more complex and of a higher order. There are various levels of seniority among the monks. The young lama begins at the bottom and tries to work his way up to being the Dorje Lopon.

The daily routine of a lama will depend on whether he is a village priest—a lama who lives in the village but has to visit the monastery regularly—a resident in a monastery, or a hermit monk. As a village priest he must perform all the daily rituals and perform any priestly service required by the villagers. As a monastic lama he has to perform many more ceremonial rituals throughout the day and attend the religious assemblies that are held at regular intervals. As a hermit he practices mortifications of the flesh all day long and spends time in deep meditation in solitary places.

Young lamas at Lachung school

LEGEND OF THE BLACK HAT DANCE

Long, long ago Tibet was ruled by a great King Ral-pa-chan. He was a devout Buddhist and during his reign many new monasteries were built. But he had a wicked brother who hated Buddhists and so had the King assassinated. The wicked Lang Dar-ma then came to the throne, persecuting lamas and destroying Buddhist monasteries.

A young Buddhist monk meditating in a secluded cave took pity on the King for all the sins he was collecting. He dressed himself in a cloak that was black on the outside and white on the inside and mounted a white charger which he painted black with charcoal. He then donned a wonderful black hat with a broad brim and galloped off to meet the King. When he was within sight of the king he pretended to do obeisance by bowing three times. On the first bow he bent his bow, on the second he fitted the arrow and on the third he drew his bow and let the arrow fly. The king was killed and the lama cried out, "I am the Black yeshe and when anybody wants to kill a wicked king let him do it as I have!" He then rode away as fast as he could. News of the King's assassination spread, and the royal soldiers gave chase to

Black hat dancers at the Phodang festival

the lama. But he outwitted them all by washing away the charcoal on his steed as he crossed a stream and turning his cloak inside out: he was now all white! To this day the bravery of the black hatted lama is celebrated in the annual dance of the Black Hats.

Once qualified, lamas assume an extremely important role in society. Their services are required at every ceremony from birth until death. They have special duties during the many festivals that dot the Buddhist calendar. And in addition their services are required throughout the year for exorcising evil spirits, curing illnesses and invoking the blessings of the good spirits. Lamas are revered by society and most Bhutia homes have a room kept ready for any visiting lama.

Lamas may retire to the Takphus or solitary caves for intense prayer and meditation; they also worship at the Lhakangs or prayer halls, and the gompas or the monasteries proper. The earliest monasteries were those built near Yoksam. Within a few decades nearly every village had its own monastery, each commanding a vantage point and easily the most impressive structure in the village. The monasteries were not just places of worship but became the centres for education and the cultural hub of the area. They were the sponsors and preservers of art, and the training centre for artists and musicians. Few monasteries had land holdings and so were supported by generous donations from Lepchas and Bhutias.

Gompas are built on a hill and face east. The monastic buildings are clustered around the central hall or temple. The outer buildings are dormitories for the monks and are like ordinary houses in Sikkim. There are more than 190 gompas and lhakangs in Sikkim.

OF PRAYER WHEEL AND ROSARY

Iconography is man's symbolic representation of the divine. Since mortal vision cannot fully comprehend the divine, he must express it in highly stylized symbolic form. Tibetan Buddhism, especially, has an incredible iconography that has emerged from the visionary experiences of saints and mystics. Some of the most important icons among the thousands that constitute the Tibetan Buddhism iconography in its entirety are the chorten, or stupas enshrining relics, the four animals and the three objects, the Eight Auspicious Signs, the Viswavajra, the Wheel of Life, representations of the Buddha, the Bodhisattvas and saints, the Goddess Dolma and the Tantric figure, Dechog.

Thankas, Prayer Flags, Prayer Wheels and Rosaries are the common prayer objects among the Buddhists in Sikkim. Prayer Wheels are cylinders with prayers (such as the holy Buddhist chant, *"Om Mane Padme Hum"*) inscribed on them which can be turned. Huge barrel-like prayer wheels line the outer walls of the temple in the gompas and miniature versions are carried around by lamas and devout Buddhists. The action of turning the prayer wheel and chanting the prayers is a symbolic imitation of the Buddha's turning the Wheel of Law after his first sermon.

A common sight on the Sikkim landscape are white flags fluttering in the breeze atop tall poles. These may be at the entrance of monasteries and in the grounds of private houses. These are prayer flag that indicate an individual's or community's offer of a special prayer. They could be square or oblong and of different designs, each of which have different significance. A prayer flag is planted ritualistically with the services of a lama on auspicious occasions, at the time of death, for good luck, to drive away illness or misfortune.

A thanka painting

The Wheel of Life

This is one of the most graphic expositions of one of the fundamental laws of Buddhism: man is entrapped in recurring cycles of rebirth with their attendant suffering. The wheel is a large disc held in the clutches of a monster, his head overtopping the whole. He symbolizes the human desire to cling to worldly existence. The Wheel is divided into compartments representing the various worlds, the hells, the heavens and the linked chain of causes of rebirth. At the centre are the three original sins of lust, anger and stupidity.

THE TALE OF GURU PADMASAMBHAVA

King Khri-Srong-Ide-btsan (775-797) of Tibet wanted to build the first monastery in the country. But it was not to be: vicious local demons unleashed floods and famine in the area. The King then requested Padmasambhava, a Tantric mystic who was a native of Udayana in north-west of India, to come to Tibet and drive away the demons. This the Guru did, vanquishing and converting them with his thunderbolt and Mahayana spells. He then helped build the monastery and established the first community of lamas. During his wanderings around Tibet he visited Sikkim and consecrated the land, predicting that Buddhism would come here centuries later. He also hid many of the secret Buddhist texts in the lakes and caves of Sikkim declaring that in the future only the most holy and learned of monks would find them and reveal them to the world. Guru Padmasambhava, also known as the Guru Rimpoche, is worshipped as the second Buddha in Sikkim and Tibet.

OTHER RELIGIONS

The entire Lepcha community in Sikkim is now Buddhist, but religion they practise is, in reality, a mixture of Buddhism and the ancient shamanistic religion of their early ancestors. Apart from its animism, the worship of ancestors is important for the Lepcha and every household has its personal deities and every individual his or her personal moongs or spirits. Animal sacrifice and invocation characterize Lepcha rituals which are presided over by the priest, called the Mun or Bonthing. The Mun is said to have special gifts and powers, being possessed by certain spirits. He knows the scriptures and legends and is crucial for any ceremony.

The Limbus are also called the Yakthungbas and their oral records show them to have strong links with the Lepchas. They have their own creation myth and peculiar customs and laws. Their distinctive religion has its own pantheon of gods and goddesses and priests called phedangmas, yebas and the female yemas. The priests are believed to have been created to counteract and control the evil forces which were unleashed along with good at the time of creation and, consequently, they are prominent members of Limbu society and crucial for all ceremonies, divinations, sacrifices and exorcisms.

Among the Nepalese, mostly Hindu, institutionalized religion is tempered with tribal beliefs. Hinduism has complex metaphysical dimensions accompanied with detailed rituals and ceremonies which pay homage to the vast and varied pantheon of gods and goddesses such as Shiva, Lakshmi, Ganesa, Durga and Kali. At the core of Hindu philosophy, however, is the concept of karma (duty), the acceptance of reincarnation, the belief that all worldly things are illusory (maya) and the hope of attaining moksha or freedom from rebirth.

The lives of the Hindu Nepali population in Sikkim follow the patterns which govern lives of Hindus in other parts of India, but a parallel religion of shamanism, indigenous to the Nepalese, co-exists with their Hindu beliefs. According to these tribal beliefs, spirits dwell in all animate and inanimate objects and may bring ill-luck to a person or community or even possess an individual. In that case the services of a jhankari must be engaged. The jhankari can be an ordinary bank clerk, but is thought to have the power to exorcise evil spirits and witches (boksas and boksis). The jhankaris do their main pujas during full moon. The belief in this cult is quite widespread among the Nepalese and even in urban areas, in the middle of the night, you could hear chants and drum beats that signal a jhankari performing a ceremony.

Christianity came to Sikkim at the end of the nineteenth century with missionaries from Scotland. The Scottish mission was established in Kalimpong and missionaries travelled deep into the interior of Sikkim. A small section of the Lepchas were converted, but even devout converts did not completely forsake their traditional faith and Christian Lepchas continue to follow many of the tribal beliefs. The missionaries opened schools; in Gangtok one of the largest girls' school belongs to the Scottish mission. Gangtok has three churches, the Scottish Mission Church, Church of North India and the Catholic Church. There is also a small number of the Sikkim population, almost all being migrants from Bihar, who are Muslim.

A bonthing performs a religious rite at Passanding village in the Lepcha sanctuary of Dzongu

RITES AND CEREMONIES

For Hindu Nepalese and Bhutia housewives alike, numerous fasts and offerings must be observed throughout the year. Many communities have complex rites of passage to signal the entry of an individual into adult life; still others, like the Newars, mark the various stages of old age. And certain journeys, too, are ritualized, especially those immediately preceding or following marriage. But of course, it is the three preeminent stages in human life—birth, marriage and death—that are marked with the most elaborate rituals by all communities.

One of the most endearing birth customs must be the one that is still practised among some Lepcha families: at its birth feast the Lepcha baby is given a tiny snail shell to wear around its wrist. This is the soul's refuge when the baby is asleep and the soul has gone wandering; for like its owner, the soul cannot move fast and so should it be pursued by a demon it may not be able to re-enter the body in time. But it can crawl into the shell for protection, safe from the demon which cannot enter the shell.

Weddings are joyful affairs, with much feasting, drinking, merrymaking and usually continue for a few days. Bride price is a common custom and may be paid in cash or kind. One of the most ritualistic wedding ceremonies is conducted by the Lepchas who combine rites of their ancient religion with Buddhist ritual.

Death marks the soul's journey into another realm, and its safe passage is ensured by much pomp and ceremony. The mourning period varies from four days among the Limbus, thirteen days among the Hindu Nepalese communities to 49 days among Buddhist communities. Cremation is the most common form of corpse disposal, but burial is popular among Buddhists and Lepchas, the latter being also known to dispose of the body by throwing it into the river.

Offerings at Hotel Tibet, Gangtok on the occasion of Tibetan New Year

Monasteries of Sikkim

Located deep in the Dzongu area, this is the most inaccessible of Sikkim's monasteries. According to legend, an incarnation of Lhatsun Chenpo had the premonition of a Nepalese invasion and ordered all the treasures of the various monasteries to be transferred to Tolung where they would be difficult to reach. Consequently, the monastery has an amazing collection of monastic art, including some of the oldest thankas in Sikkim. The collection also includes ancient saddles, saddle cloths, thigh bone trumpets, breastplates, circlets and armlets. Every three years this collection is taken out, and pilgrims visit from great distances for a glimpse.

Tolung

Tashiding was built in 1716 by Pedi Wangmo, Chador Namgyal's half sister, on the spot supposed to have been consecrated by Guru Rimpoche. Legend has it that the Guru shot an arrow and vowed to meditate where it fell. The arrow dropped on the spot where the monastery stands now. This gompa has a picturesque, peaceful location between the Ratong and Rangit rivers on a hill top and is surrounded by deep valleys. It is second only to Pemayangtse in sacredness for the Nyingma sect. Its chorten is considered the most holy in Sikkim and is said to have been built by Lhatsun Chenpo. The Bum-chu festival is peculiar to Tashiding.

PHENSANG: The Phensang monastery was built in 1721 by the third incarnation of Lhatsun Chenpo, Lama Jigm Pawo. It was completely gutted by a devastating fire 1947 but was restored the following year due to the support of the laity and the devotion of the monks. It ha 300 monks of the Nyingma sect and the annual chaam i held two days before Losoong.

Pemayangtse, the Perfect Sublime Lotus, is a magnificent monastery in western Sikkim commanding one of the finest views of the Kangchendzonga range. It was built during the reign of the third Chogyal, Chador Namgyal, in 1705 on the spot where Lhatsun Chenpo had earlier erected a small shrine. It is Sikkim's most respected monastery and all the Nyingma monasteries are subordinate to it. It possesses exquisite works of art and sculpture.
There are around 108 monks in the monastery and traditionlly, they must belong to leading Bhutia families of Sikkim. In the past the head monk had the honour of crowning the Chogyals of Sikkim and even today the dances in honour of Kangchendzonga and the Pang Lhabsol dances are performed in the palace temple in Gangtok by the monks of this monastery. During the annual chaams held at this monastery pilgrims, visit from all over Sikkim.

Tashiding

Pemayangtse

Ralong

This Kargyupa monastery in south Sikkim was built after the return of the fourth Chogyal from a pilgrimage to Tibet. The Karmapa performed a blessing ceremony on its completion, in Tsurphu, Tibet, and grains of ri from his far away ceremony ar said to have fallen on the ground at Ralong. The monastery has recently been rebuilt and has about a hundre monks. The annual chaams are held two days before Losoong

Gayzing

Namchi

Rangit River

Melli

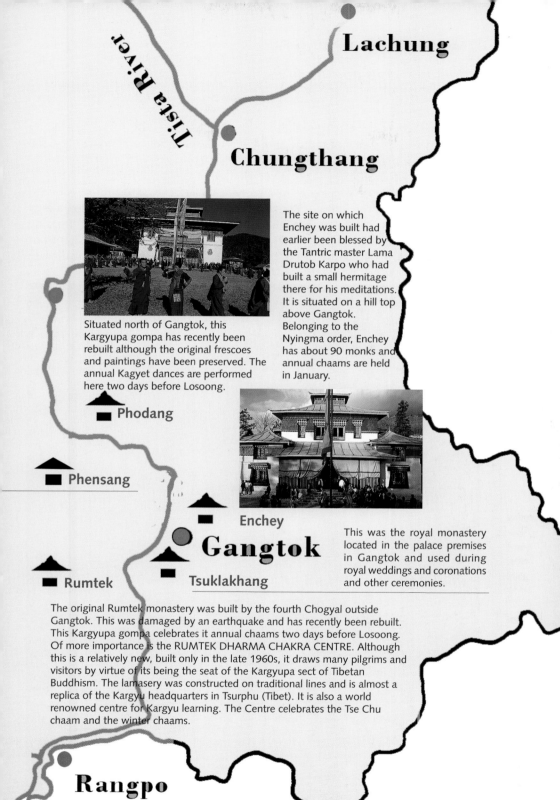

Lachung

Tista River

Chungthang

The site on which Enchey was built had earlier been blessed by the Tantric master Lama Drutob Karpo who had built a small hermitage there for his meditations. It is situated on a hill top above Gangtok. Belonging to the Nyingma order, Enchey has about 90 monks and annual chaams are held in January.

Situated north of Gangtok, this Kargyupa gompa has recently been rebuilt although the original frescoes and paintings have been preserved. The annual Kagyet dances are performed here two days before Losoong.

Phodang

Phensang

Enchey

Rumtek

Gangtok

Tsuklakhang

This was the royal monastery located in the palace premises in Gangtok and used during royal weddings and coronations and other ceremonies.

The original Rumtek monastery was built by the fourth Chogyal outside Gangtok. This was damaged by an earthquake and has recently been rebuilt. This Kargyupa gompa celebrates it annual chaams two days before Losoong. Of more importance is the RUMTEK DHARMA CHAKRA CENTRE. Although this is a relatively new, built only in the late 1960s, it draws many pilgrims and visitors by virtue of its being the seat of the Kargyupa sect of Tibetan Buddhism. The lamasery was constructed on traditional lines and is almost a replica of the Kargyu headquarters in Tsurphu (Tibet). It is also a world renowned centre for Kargyu learning. The Centre celebrates the Tse Chu chaam and the winter chaams.

Rangpo

"Throughout Sikkim, we were roused each morning at day break by this wild music... To me it was deeply impressive, awakening me so effectually to the strangeness of the wild land in which I was wandering."

Himalayan Journals by Sir Joseph Dalton Hooker

In a land where stars are thought to be the laughter of Gods frozen for eternity on the face of heaven, myths and legends are central to everyday life and permeate the daily existence of the people. Even today, life is modulated by ancient rhythms and reality is perceived through the filter of myth.

A rich storehouse of legends existed with the Lepchas and further enriched with the coming of the Bhutias. They brought with them the lore and mythology of Tibetan Buddhism—tales of the Buddha, of demons and deities, of amazing deeds by virtuous lamas. And finally, the Nepalese contributed their strands of Hindu mythology, tales from their primitive religions and legends of mighty heroes to the multi-variegated tapestry of Sikkimese folk tales.

A Storied Land

Offerings of butter lamps and fruits to Lord Buddha on the Lhabab Duechen festival

Written literature in all communities is restricted to religious writings. The earliest extant Lepcha literature consists of Namthars or religious books written by Buddhist monks to help in spreading their religion among the Lepchas. Pre-eminent among these is the Tashay Sung—a biography of the great Guru Padmasambhava. A remarkable feature of these Namthars is that they are not mechanical translations of the original Tibetan works: instead, they are transcreations of the originals into a Lepcha context, no doubt to make the matter more accessible and interesting for the intended audience.

Tibetan religious literature can be found in the libraries of the monasteries. The two great lamaic encyclopedias are the Kangyur or Commandments and the Tengyur or Commentaries. The Kangyur fills a hundred volumes of a thousand pages each. These are translations from Sanskrit and Chinese originals. Libraries also possess legendary accounts of the many Buddhist saints and mystics as well as books on medicine and astrological calculation.

The Dancer's Crown

The Lepchas believe that their musical gifts and dancing skills are gifts from heaven and these arts are a bridge between earth and heaven. They relate how the God of music and dance, Na-rok-Rom, once came down and joined the singing and dancing which was being performed at a Lepcha village. So pleased was he by the performance that he gifted the Lepchas with ten musical instruments and placed his own crown made of feathers from a heavenly bird on the head of the leading dancer. The Lepchas still worship the dancer's crown before putting it on to perform a dance, and if the crown should fall off it is considered to be a very bad omen.

SONG AND DANCE

Each ethnic group has an impressive array of folk songs and dances and there is one to suit every occasion. Songs can be simple ditties on topical themes like those sung at wedding feasts or they may be religious chants. Dances, too, can vary from informal rhythmic movements during

Bardo Lhamsol or the " long horns" are played at Enchey monastery in Gangtok during the annual dances

festive gatherings such as a birth feast or a wedding to the highly stylized dance dramas held on Buddhist festivals.

Songs are based on folklore and myths and are sung at feasts, weddings, harvest celebrations and almost all joyful occasions. Often there is a extempore quality to the songs with topical allusions being interpolated to suit the occasion. The Damai have a special wedding song known as shilok and the Tamang have a rich tradition of folk songs known as jougi. Bhailo and Dewsi are also traditional Nepalese songs sung during Dasai and Tihar.

All communities play a variety of wind, percussion and stringed instruments: indigenous musical instruments abound. In the monasteries there is a special grade of lamas whose duty it is to play the various musical instruments such as the the long trumpet-like pak-doong. The Bhutias

Making yak cheese and butter in a tent at Naku near the Tibet border

enjoy strumming on the stringed dram-nye. Among the Nepalese, too, there are a number of indigenous instruments. The Limbus, for instance, have the Kay and the nagare (kettle drum) and the Tamangs have a special tambourine called domphu. The Damais, who are traditionally musicians, have the Naumata Baja or nine-instrument orchestra.

Dances, usually performed by both men and women, are characterized by vigour and rhythm. The most spectacular are the dances performed during various Buddhist festivals. At religious festivals Lepchas dance their distinctive Kagyet dance.

AND THEN SOME HOT SOUP AND CHHANG

Except for the Brahmans of the Nepalese community, Sikkimese people are not usually vegetarian. Pork is almost a staple and other than in some

sections of the Hindu Nepalese community, beef is also popular. While the poor may not be able to afford meat on a regular basis, for those who are reasonably well-off, meat is considered essential at the main meal of the day. Rice and wheat form the staple cereals, but millet, barley, maize, buckwheat and a variety of pulses are also common. Chicken and eggs are not only regular dietary items but are also important for festive meals. Sikkimese tea is quite different from the tea most tea-drinkers know. Tea leaves and hot water are churned with butter and salt and it is considered ready to drink when no grease remains floating on the surface.

Potatoes and onion are everyday fare, while some of the more exotic vegetables include arrowroot, bamboo shoots, mushrooms, a bitter orchid known as nakami and a tasty fern called Ningro. For the Lepchas, with their remarkable knowledge of the forests and plants, the array of plants they can consume is almost endless since they can identify an amazing variety of ferns, shoots, berries, fungi, tubers and leaves which are edible.

Yak milk, together with butter and cheese (churpi) made from this milk is an important source of nourishment for the Bhutia yak herders who live in the high altitudes. Churpi can be eaten both fresh and dried. In the form of fresh cheese it tastes not unlike soybean curd and is often used in soups or pickles. Cubes of dried churpi are chewed like chewing gum to keep the body warm.

While rice, dal and meat is the basic everyday fare in most Sikkimese homes, the most popular meal, for the Sikkimese and tourists consists of momos and thukpa. Few meals can be more satisfying at the end of hard day's trekking than a steaming plate of momos. These steamed dumplings are filled with pork or beef mince and finely chopped seasonings such as spring onions. Thukpa—a wholesome broth with vegetables and rice or egg noodles— accompanies the momos. A variety of sauces such as the red sauce — a fiery compound of crushed garlic, red chili and other spices — is served as garnish. Vegetarian momos, known as zino yenten, can also be had.

BUDDHIST CALENDAR

The Tibetan calendar plots time in ten-month years which proceed in sixty-year cycles. Each year is a combination of an animal, an element and a gender. The mouse ox, tiger, hare, dragon, serpent, horse, sheep, monkey, bird, dog, hog, in that order constitute the animals. The order of elements is wood, fire, earth, iron, water. Each element is given a pair of animals, the first being considered male, the second, female.

In Bhutia kitchens, along with momos and thukpa, another favourite is ghyatuk (a noodle soup) and khudi (paper-thin, crisp pancakes made of buckwheat). On ceremonial occasions the sweet khabse (fried dough cookies) and the savoury fongui amcho are common features. Winter is the season for preserving meat in a variety of forms and on a scale that will ensure a supply through most of the following months.

Dried meat, blood sausages and many other such traditional delicacies are made in the Bhutia kitchens at this time.

Nepalese specialties include the highly-spiced Nepalese curry, potatoes cooked with sesame seeds, eggs cooked whole in a dry curry form and egg noodles—cooked in turmeric and eaten with potato curry—and a variety of pickles and spicy sauces.

The winter haat at Lall Market, Gangtok

Food is washed down with chang, the local brew that accompanies at least one of the day's meals. This beer is brewed by almost everyone in Sikkim. It is usually prepared from wheat, barley or millet seeds, but rice and a variety of wild plants such as elephant creepers and yams are also used at times. The seeds are soaked for two nights, then husked and washed and the water drained off. The seeds remain in the vessel for a few hours and are then spread out on a mat. When cooled they are mixed with various spices and the mixture is covered and allowed to ferment for at least forty-eight hours. The resultant beer is drunk warm from a bamboo through a thin bamboo straw or pipsey with the invocation,"Tashi Delek!".

A Tibetan food stall at Gangtok

Celebrating the Gods

Lamas at the ceremonial winter dances at Rumtek

Barely a month goes by in Sikkim without a festival being celebrated. This is hardly surprising given the state's rich ethnic diversity and multi-cultural society. Hindu and Buddhist scriptural beliefs intermingled with colourful tribal customs give Sikkim a breathtaking array of feasts and festivals. Many are of a religious nature—the Saga Dawa, the Bum-Chu and the Drukpa-Tsechi of the Buddhists; the Dasai and Maghey Sankranti of the Hindu Nepalese community; the Lepcha feast of the river Gods. Yet others are secular, celebrating the New Year, the harvest or familial ties such as the Nepalese Bhai Tika.

Festivals are a time for rejoicing and relaxation from daily chores and add colour to this beautiful land. They are also a time for renewing the bonds of the community. Through them ancient traditions are kept alive and cultures are reinvigorated as the young are initiated into the rites and customs of their heritage so that they may in turn pass this knowledge to the next generation, thereby ensuring the continuity of communal identity. And while each community celebrates its festivals in a distinct manner, participation in each others' festivals is the accepted norm.

Lepcha Festivals

Despite their conversion to Buddhism, Lepchas continue to celebrate many of their ancient festivals. These are usually occasions for great feasting, sometimes lasting as long as three nights. Not surprisingly, therefore, most of the festivals take place in the autumn and winter months when the harvest has been brought in and it is a time of plenty. Namsoong and the Feast of the River Gods are two big Lepcha festivals.

NAMSOONG OR NAMBUN: This festival celebrates the harvest and the advent of the New Year. It falls on the tenth month of the Tibetan calendar (corresponding to December). People gather to enjoy the harvest and pray for a prosperous New Year.

THE FEAST OF THE RIVER GODS: The confluence of the Tista and the Rangit rivers is a holy spot for the Lepchas. And every year, during December-January, the Lepchas gather here from distant places to celebrate the feast of the river gods. Young girls and boys take a dip in the river then sing and dance late into the night, celebrating the great love of these two rivers.

Nepalese Festivals

The major Nepalese festivals are festivals of the Hindu calendar. However, the Nepalese add their own colour to these festivals so that their celebration in Sikkim is not identical to their observation in the plains, and thus unique.

DASAI OR VIJAY DASAMI: This festival generally falls during the month of October and celebrates the slaying of the demon Mahisasura by Goddess Durga—symbolic of the destruction of evil by the forces of good. While this is the same as the Dussehra festival observed in other parts of India, the Nepalese have added the tika ceremony— a holy sign of blessing, usually a mixture of curd, rice and vermillion, put on by the elders of the family on the foreheads of the younger members.

TIHAR: Corresponding to the Diwali festival in other parts of India, this is generally celebrated a fortnight after Dasai and symbolizes the return of the epic hero Rama from his fourteen-year exile. According to legend he reached his kingdom during the new moon and hence people lighted lamps to dispel the darkness. The Nepalese celebrate this festival for five days and during this time groups of boys known as Daosi visit neighboring houses singing dewsi for small tips.

CHAITE DASAIN: This marks the birth of Rama and is celebrated as the Nepalese New Year. The festival falls during April.

BHAI TIKA: Usually celebrated on the fifth day of Tihar —a ceremony during which sisters put sandalwood tika on their brothers' forehead and bless them with a long life and happiness.

MAGHEY SANKRANTI: Held in January, this is a major secular festival for the Nepalese and celebrates the change of seasons as the sun shifts towards the Tropic of Cancer. During the ceremony, a bathing festival called Makkar is observed, when people take a dip at the confluence of the Tista and Rangit. Traditionally, this bathing commemorates the time when Gurkha soldiers bathed at the confluence to wash away the blood stains after a victorious battle.

Buddhist Festivals

The monasteries are the venue for the Buddhist festivals which, in terms of spectacle and grandeur, are unmatched. The Buddhist calendar is studded with many festivals and ceremonies throughout the year and many are celebrated in Sikkim with great pomp and splendour. The monasteries are the venues of these celebrations and people come from distant places to witness them. Pang Lhabsol, Lhabab Deuchen, Drukpa Tsechi, Saga Dawa, Losar, Losoong, Bum-chu —these are major Buddhist festivals of Sikkim. At many of these festivals, chaams are performed. These are masked dance dramas with liturgical significance, performed in the monasteries by monks. The ornate masks and costumes are of resplendent colour and the dances are finely choreographed sequences requiring skill, training and vigour. (See also 'Monasteries in the Mountains' for more on festivals of the Buddhists.)

DRUKPA TSECHI: The festival celebrates Buddha's preaching of the first sermon at Sarnath. It falls on the 4th day of the 6th Tibetan month (roughly, August). In Gangtok it is marked by prayers at the Deer Park. And in Muguthang, situated in the remote Lhonak in north Sikkim, there are prayers followed by a yak race.

BUM-CHU: This festival is celebrated at Tashiding in January/February. During this festival, the pot containing the holy water is opened by the lamas. The level of water in the pot foretells the future of the coming year: brimful foretells bloodshed and disturbances; if the pot is almost dry famine is predicted; and if the pot is half-full then it promises a year of peace and prosperity. A part of the holy water is distributed among the pilgrims and then the pot is sealed until the next year.

TSE-CHU: This is an important chaam of the Rumtek Dharma Chakra Centre. It falls on the tenth day of the fifth Tibetan month. It presents the eight manifestations of the Guru Rimpoche. The masked dances celebrate various episodes from his life and his battle against the demons of the Bon tradition.

THE KAGYET DANCE: This dance is performed two days before Losoong at Tsuklakhang and are also celebrated at Phodang. This religious dance-drama enacts various themes from the Buddhist mythologies and culminates with the burning of effigies made of flour, wood and paper symbolizing the destruction of evil by the forces of good. The participants are always monks from the monastery and the performance is accompanied by liturgical music and chanting. Prior to the dance prayers are held in the chapel and for the thousands who flock to see the dance, seeing the spectacle is itself an act of worship as well as participation in the exorcising of evil and ushering in a prosperous new year. The solemn nature of the dances is interspersed with comic relief provided by prancing jesters.

PANG LHABSOL: This festival is unique to Sikkim and celebrates the consecration of Mount Kangchendzonga into Buddhist religion. It is also a commemoration of the blood brotherhood sworn between the Lepchas and the Bhutias at Kabi. The chaams which accompany this festival are spectacular, and the warrior dance or pangtoed dance especially is superbly choreographed. Kangchendzonga is represented as wearing a red mask wreathed with five human skulls, on top of which are planted flags and riding a snow lion. Yabdu, the mountain's chief commander, wears a black mask. The warriors who accompany them wear the traditional Sikkimese battle dress with helmets, shields and swords. The dramatic entry of Mahakala (the protector of Dharma) is one of the highlights of the dance. It is Mahakala who commands Kangchendzonga and Yabdu to defend the faith and bring peace and prosperity to Sikkim. A week prior to the chaams, the lamas of Pemayangtse monastery offer prayers to Kangchendzonga asking it to protect the land and look after the people. This festival is held on the fifteenth day of the seventh month of the Tibetan calendar, corresponding to late August/early September.

SAGA DAWA: The fourth month of the Tibetan calendar (approximately corresponding to early May), is an auspicious month for the Sikkimese Buddhists and prayers are held throughout the period in various monasteries. On the full moon of this month, the Buddha is supposed to have been born, attained Buddhahood and achieved Nirvana. This is the day of the main celebration. A colourful processions of monks go around the major thoroughfares of Gangtok with the holy Kangyur texts. Similar processions, invariably beginning from the gompas, are taken out in the villages.

LOSOONG: This is a festival marked with great gaiety. The Black Hat dances take place at this festival commemorating the victory of good over evil. These chaams are held at Enchey, Ralong, Phodang and Rumtek monasteries two days prior to Losoong.

LOSAR: This is the Tibetan new year and is celebrated with festivities and chaams depicting the ritualized destruction of evil by good being performed at Pemayangtse and the Rumtek Dharma Chakra.

LHABAB DEUCHEN: This festival symbolizes the descent of the Buddha from the 33rd heaven after visiting his mother to convert her to the Dharma. It falls on the 22nd day of the 9th month of the Tibetan calendar.

A porter at Lall Market Gangtok

Overleaf: A boy examines a video poster on the way to Lall Market, Gangtok

Gangtok, The Capital

· ·

"God made the country, and man made the town."
— *The Task, by Cowper*

During my childhood years in Darjeeling, I never had the opportunity to visit Gangtok. I had read about the capital of Sikkim, on the trade route between Tibet and Kalimpong. During the 1940s and '50s, traders from Tibet used to travel from Lhasa across the Chumbi valley and reach Gangtok. They used to cross the Nathu La and Jelep La passes on their way to the Sikkimese capital, their pack ponies laden with wool, coral, chinese brocade and pearls. In return they took back salt, guns, broadcloth and watches to Tibet. Enthralled with fantastic images of these ancient travellers, I dreamt of going to Gangtok.

I first visited Gangtok in 1986. By this time, a new era had been ushered in. Massive aid from India, which had annexed it in 1975, a lenient tax structure and heavy government subsidies resulted in investments in industries, tie-ups with multinational business houses and the establishment of a large and moneyed middle class. Brand new Maruti Gypsies whizzed along the roads, buildings were being constructed in a mish mash of architectural styles. Concrete monstrosities had sprung up in different parts of a town where once the blue curved roofs of official buildings offset the red–topped private homes.

The young Sikkimese have a fascination for films featuring martial arts. On the way to Lall Market, a video parlours proclaims the 'Legacy of Riga' and screens a film featuring 'Brandon Lee, son of Bruce Lee'. Rock music and 'Minkaa Dragon' concerts are all the rage. Electronic goods from abroad fill the shelves marked with staggering price tags to suit the shopping culture of the new Sikkimese. Fashions too have taken on an integrated look. With a return to ethnic tastes, khos and honjus are streamlined to synchronize with unisex jeans and the salwar kameez.

And yet, tradition dies hard. On Sundays, the weekly haat is held at Lall Market when the capital comes to the village. Busteewallas (villagers), Yap Las and Chum Las (the landed gentry) trudge in from over the hills and far way to buy and sell. It is in Lall Market on Sundays that the pulse of Sikkim throbs, and the congregation of races that have mingled in Sikkim meets at the bazaar.

A laughing Nepali women weighs out rice while her petite rosy cheeked Lepcha neighbour arranges her long skirts to sit comfortably behind her pile of fern fronds and mushrooms. A gaunt Tibetan Khamba chews tobacco in phlegmatic rumination while hard bargaining goes on over his second hand woollens and tracksuits. Blocks of Tibetan tea, fresh cheese and butter, edible greens of every description, chillies, tomatoes, brinjals and carrots sit in colourful heaps.

In Gangtok, I used to visit the home of the Densapas, the leaders of the Bhutia-Lepchas, the original people of Sikkim. Jigdal Densapa, one of the brothers, had been the Secretary to the Chogyal of Sikkim in the Durbar days. Fiercely patriotic, scrupulously honest and an old-fashioned gentleman, he used to put up with my demands with good-humoured tolerance. Visits to different parts of Sikkim had been organised with his help and infrastructure. His younger brother Thinlay became a good friend of mine and we would wander around Gangtok in his white Gypsy with music blaring through the loudspeakers.

The Sikkimese are great football fans and in October every year, the Governor's Gold Cup Football tournament is held at the Paljor Stadium. Outstation teams are invited from all over India and during those two weeks, the entire capital is in the grip of football fever. The Secretariat closes early, schoolchildren rush after school to the matches. On one occasion, the final coincided with the birthday celebrations of the charismatic Nar Bahadur Bhandari, then Sikkim's Chief Minister. A huge cake was presented to him by the Sikkim Football Association and amidst much cheers and balloons, the birthday party was celebrated at the stadium.

In March 1987, I was at Gayzing when I heard the Queen Mother of Sikkim had passed away. Jigdal Densapa had sent a message to the District Collector, T.P.Ghimiray, asking for the lamas of Pemayangtse monastery to leave for the Palace immediately. I decided to attend the funeral and left for Gangtok.

I reached Tsuklakhang early in the morning. The Sikkim Government had declared the day of the funeral a holiday. The lamas had been praying day and night at the Tsuklakhang monastery for the departed soul. The

Jigdal Densapa at his Tashiling office in Gangtok

monastery was surrounded by crowds waiting to pay their last respects. Lamas had come from different monasteries all over Sikkim. White khadas were piled in a mountain like hump at the entrance of the monastery. Ministers and schoolchildren, lamas and shopkeepers, bureaucrats and businessmen were all at Tsuklakhang. It felt as though the entire town had turned up to see the cortege off. The funeral had melded caste and creed, religion and customs. Bhutia–Lepchas and Nepalis walked side by side as the cortege left for Lukshyama Hill where members of the Royal family were cremated. It seemed that for a brief moment Gangtok was suspended in time and the clock had gone back to the time when Sikkim was a monarchy.

On my visit to Sikkim in 1992, I spent a couple of days in Gangtok. I noticed with alarm the mushrooming of buildings in every nook and cranny of the town. Past Tadong and Deorali, the whole hill side was dotted with buildings, most of them unfinished. They were ugly concrete constructions, often three to four storeys high with the

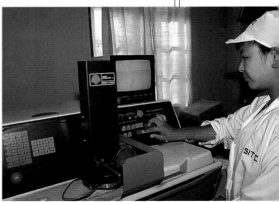

Working with precision instruments at the Sikkim Time Corporation factory at Tadong

Chidren of Pelling school take out a victory procession to celebrate the recognition of the Nepali language by the Indian constitution

Former Sikkim Chief Minister Nar Bahadur Bhandari cuts his birthday cake at the Governor's Gold Cup football final at Paljor Stadium Gangtok

Modern high-rise buildings cover the hillside at Deorali, a suburb of Gangtok

inevitable dish antennas on the rooftops. Television soaps like *Santa Barbara* and *The Bold and the Beautiful* seemed to have mesmerized the town. Massive arches and overbridges had been constructed near the hospital and the bazaar.

Sikkim was celebrating the 'recognition' of the Nepali language by the Central Government. Chief Minister Bhandari had worked for this recognition for many years—his posters and enormous cut-outs adorned different parts of the capital. Victory processions were taken out by the ebullient youth, cries of `Nar Bahadur Zindabad' rang through the town.

In the evening, I walked across to Cherry Banks. Thinlay was tending his roses in the garden. He showed me the new rockery he was planning to build against the hillside. From the Densapa home there is a view over the entire town. The hillside once dotted with carefully constructed cottages had become any other sprawling modern Indian hill town. I mentioned this to Thinlay.

" With money pouring in, who's to stop buildings from being constructed," he retorted without looking up, as he watered another rose bush.

As dusk fell, we looked upon the lights of Rumtek across the valley. I had heard in Gangtok that the new Karmapa had been found discovered in Kham province of Tibet. He was a child, barely eight years old. I asked Thinlay whether the Chinese Government would permit him to come to Sikkim.

"Who can say," he replied, "it depends on the negotiation between the Indians and the Chinese."

By 1994, Sikkim was on the tourist map of India. Government had relaxed the restrictions for foreign tourists visiting the state and as a result, permits were now merely a formality. The barren north had been opened to tourists in groups upto Yumthang valley and resorts like Snow Lion Mountain resort were catering to visitors on conducted tours. On the former trade route to Nathu la, Tsangu Lake was on every visitor's itinerary—around thirty to forty jeeps laden with visitors visit Tsangu daily from Gangtok during the season to experience the snow. The Government had changed and a young and dynamic Chief Minister, Pawan Chamling from Namchi was confident of leading Sikkim "into the twenty first century".

Sitting in the Cherry Banks garden, I wondered whether the annexation had integrated Sikkim into the Indian mainstream. Despite all the changes and apparent homogenizing, to me Sikkim still retained its enchanting blend of cultures and time zones.

Shiv Shankar from the plains of Bihar runs a sweet meat shop in Gangtok bazaar

(Pages 120-121): The funeral cortege of the Queen Mother of Sikkim near the Palace

(Pages 122-123): A dreary monsoon day at Gangtok

Trekking an

Kangchendzonga (left) and Pandim (right) with the chortens at Dablakhang

Previous page: A shepherd treks from Tsokha to Dzongri carrying provisions for the summer

" The body roams the mountains; and the spirit is set free"

Chinese poet Hsu Hsai - k'o

Sikkim offers some of the finest trekking country in the Himalaya. As entry to the hill state was restricted for many years, trekking is not too commercialized so far. The concept of "tea h-ouse trekking", with lodges for travellers en route, which is very popular in Nepal has not yet developed in Sikkim. Even so, there are numerous trekking companies both in Gangtok and overseas which conduct group treks. Most of these run expedition-style treks with tents, porters, cooks, food and all other necessities provided for.

Seasons: The peak trekking seasons are May-June and October-November. It is possible to trek outside these seasons, but the winter months of December and January can be very cold above 3000 metres and trails are often snow bound. The monsoon months, June to September, are wet and leech infested but this is a good time to see the flowers in bloom especially on the high altitude meadows.

Adventure

THE DZONGRI/ GOECHA LA TREK

This is undoutably the most popular trek in Sikkim and famed for superb mountain views, a floral spectacle in summer, birds, and views of pristine forest. The trek passes through the Kangchendzonga National Park and trekkers have to pay park fees at Yoksam before entering the park.

Gangtok to Yoksam

This part of the journey is done by road usually in a jeep or Land Rover. It is also possible to go directly from Siliguri or Bagdogra airport in the plains to Yoksam, the route being Tista Bazaar-Melli-Jorethang-Legship-Tashiding-Yoksam; the journey time would be about the same in both instances. Visitors to the Pemayangtse monastery and Pelling can go direct to Yoksam across the valley via Rimbi, a journey that takes about two hours or so by jeep. The Sikkim Nationalised Transport bus, which used to go to Yoksam earlier has now discontinued its service because of bad roads. However, once the roads improve, service may resume. There are a number of hotels in Yoksam and accommodation is no longer a problem.
(6-7 hours)

Yoksam (1785 m) to Tsokha (3000 m)

The trail from Yoksam climbs gently out of the valley and follows the Rathong Chu river which can be heard thundering through the gorge below. The trail meanders through dense forest and crosses four bridges around fifty-minute-walks from each other. The last bridge is the longest and there is a camping spot here on the banks of the river. In the monsoon this part of the trail is inundated with leeches and salt is required to shake them off. From the fourth bridge the trail climbs steeply for an hour to the forest rest house at Bakhim which was the old halting point before trekkers huts were built at Tsokha. The Bakhim Rest House is still

A trekker makes his way through the lush monsoon forests between Yoksam and Bakhim on the Dzongri trek

used by the Himalayan Mountaineering Institute for accommodation en route to their Base camp at Chauringkhang, a days march from Dzongri. Trekkers can stay here by paying a small fee to the chowkidar. The chowkidar at Bakhim can usually rustle up some smoky tea and there is a good view from the bungalow down the valley towards Yoksam. From Bakhim, the trail climbs steeply through forests of magnolia and rhododendron to Tsokha, which takes an hour to reach. The Trekkers Hut at Tsokha has a large camping ground behind it and groups usually pitch their tents here. There are two private lodges in Tsokha which also provide accommodation.

(6-7 hours)

Tsokha (3000 m) to Dzongri (4030 m)

The trail climbs steeply through forests of rhododendron to the alp of Phidang (3650 m) and it takes around 3 hours. This is the steepest part of the trek as there is little respite in the form of descents. The clearing at Phidang is generally used as a lunch spot and in good weather the peaks can be seen across the valley. During May and June this part of the walk is exceptionally beautiful as rhododendrons in their myriad hues flower on either side of the trail. The trail evens off a bit from Phidang before it climbs again for Mon Lepcha, a pass which is a little higher than the Dzongri Trekkers Hut. On a good day Mon Lepcha commands an exceptional view of Pandim. The trail descends from Mon Lepcha before climbing again and the Dzongri Trekkers Hut soon comes into view. The distance from Phidang to Dzongri should not take more than two hours.

(5-6 hours)

Rest Day at Dzongri

It is advisable to have a rest day at Dzongri both for acclimatization as well as to savour the views of the mountains.

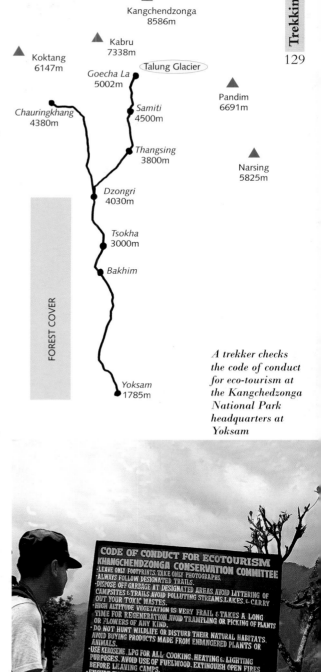

A trekker checks the code of conduct for eco-tourism at the Kangchedzonga National Park headquarters at Yoksam

Climb the hill above the bungalow—
referred to as Dzongri Top—for a
panoramic view of Kabru, Ratong,
Kangchendzonga, Koktang, Pandim,
Narsing and Jobonu. In the afternoon
walk up to the Dzongri meadows and
climb up to the ridge at Dablakhang with
the four chortens.

Dzongri (4030 m) to Thangsing (3800 m)

The trail from Dzongri passes the
bungalow and climbs up along the banks
of the river. After cresting the hill the
trail drops into the valley and then
crosses a bridge over the Prek Chu river.
During late May and June this part of
the trail is exceptionally beautiful with
the rhododendron blossoms. Thangsing
is an hours' climb from the bridge and is
located below the slopes of Pandim. This
is usually an easy day and the more
intrepid trekkers often travel to Samiti
on the same day. This is however not
recommended unless you are very well
acclimatized and fit. There is a trekkers
hut at Thangsing.
(3 to 3.5 hours)

Thangsing (3800 m) to Samiti (4500 m)

The trail from Thangsing climbs
gently up the valley and about an hour
above Thangsing you reach
Onglathang, which has a superb view
of the south face of Kangchendzonga.
Start early from Thangsing so that you
can see the view before the clouds rush
in. The trail skirts a series of moraines
and then climbs steeply to the lake. It is
usually very cold at the trekkers hut in
Samiti and afternoon snowfall is a
regular feature here especially in the
spring.
(4 to 5 hours)

**Samiti (4500 m) to Goecha La (5002 m) pass
and back to Kokchorung (3800 m)**

The climb to Goecha la begins with
a gentle gradient for about half an hour

Unseasonal spring snowfall makes the going difficult for trekkers en route from Dzongri to Thangsing

and then the real climbing starts. A rough scramble over rocks and boulders with a rise of about 400 m will bring the trekker to the top of the pass. Most trekkers leave Samiti by first light so as to reach the top by 8.30 am or so. The pass is formed by a depression between Pandim and the Kabru spurs. It overlooks the Talung valley and commands a very impressive view of the south face of Kangchendzonga. The way down is quick and the night halt is at Kokchurung, which is usually reached in the late afternoon.
(6 to 7 hours)

Kokchurung (3800 m) to Tsokha (3000 m)
It is possible to bypass Dzongri and reach Tsokha direct though many of the guides and porters do not like this route as it travels through the forest and the trail is difficult to find especially if it has snowed. Ask the chowkidar at Dzongri or Thangsing about the best route back as the trail conditions change depending on the time of the year/snowfall/rain/ landslides etc.
(5 – 6 hours)

Tsokha (3000 m) to Yoksam (2100 m)
Retrace your steps to Yoksam on the final day on the trek. The going is easier as the path is mainly downhill.
(4-5 hours)

Dzongri (4030 m) to Chauringkhang (4380 m) and back, a side-trip
It is a day's walk from Dzongri to the Himalayan Mountaineering Institute (HMI) Base Camp at Chauringkhang. The camp is located on the edge of the Ratong glacier with spectacular views of Kabru, Kabru Dome, Koktang, Ratong and Frey's Peak. A two-hour walk along the glacier leads to Dudh Pokhari with its milky white waters surrounded by peaks. The side trip to Chauringkhang would add two extra days to the trek.

Green Lakes
5050m

Zemu Glacier

Kangchendzonga

Siniolchu

FOREST COVER

Rest Camp
4500m

Yabuk
3850m

Lachen
2700m

Jakthang
3300m

THE GREEN LAKES TREK

The trek to Green Lakes, the base camp of Mount Kangchendzonga on the Zemu glacier in North Sikkim, is presently restricted. However, with the relaxation of permits by the Sikkim Government, it is expected that this area will also be thrown open to group trekkers very soon. In late spring around May and June, this is a splendid walk with a variety of flowers like rhododendrons, blue poppies, and primulas all in bloom. The mountain views are fantastic with an amphitheater of peaks with Kangchendzonga at the head of the valley. However, the Green Lakes base camp is at more than 5000 metres and so proper acclimatization is essential to avoid altitude sickness. There are no trekker's huts or bungalows along this route so any team attempting the trek

Trekkers examine the north-east face of Kangchendzonga from a high camp above Green Lakes

must be entirely self sufficient, with tents, food and porters. The route is best done in a guided group trek with proper infrastructure.

Gangtok to Lachen (2700 m)

This part of the journey on the first day will have to be covered by jeep along the North Sikkim Highway and is likely to take around 6-7 hours depending on road conditions, landslides etc.

Lachen (2700 m) to Jakthang (3300 m)

Follow the main North Sikkim Highway to Thangu proceeding north to the junction of the Lachen Chu and the Zemu Chu at Zema. After crossing the Zemu Chu by the permanent bridge, go westwards up the Zemu valley following a trail through the forest. The going in this section is usually slow as the path travels through water-logged rhododendron thickets and fallen tree

trunks rotting in the morass. Before Jakthang the path crosses the Lhonak Chu which usually has a bridge though landslides can often wreak havoc in this section of the trail. Jakthang is situated in a small meadow with a broken herdsmen's hut that makes a convenient first night's halt.

(5–6 hours)

Jakthang (3300 m) to Yabuk (3850 m)

The path to Yabuk climbs through the forest and after about three hours of steady walking you reach the snout of the Zemu glacier. Yabuk is usually reached by lunchtime and trekkers may be tempted to make it to the Rest Camp at the glacier on the same day. This is only suggested if you are properly acclimatized.

(4-5 hours)

Yabuk (3850 m) to Rest Camp (4500 m)

The path now follows the glacier of the Zemu. The trail is mainly over boulders and in parts is indistinct. The Zemu Chu rushes through the glacier and as the valley opens up the great peaks come into view. The Rest Camp is situated right opposite Siniolchu and has a fabulous view of the one of the most beautiful mountains in Sikkim. Bharal or blue sheep are often sighted on the hill opposite the Rest Camp and this is also snow leopard country. Walk slowly as the air is getting thinner and acclimatization becomes of essence.

(4-5 hours)

Rest Camp (4500 m) to Green Lakes (5050 m)

The trail from Rest Camp climbs gently up the valley. The walking pace is usually slow because of the altitude. On a clear morning this is one of the finest walks in the Himalaya rivaling the walk from Machhapuchare Base Camp to Annapurna Base Camp on the Annapurna Sanctuary trek and from

Dingboche to Chukung on the Everest Trek in Nepal.

Siniolchu, Simvu, Twins, Nepal Peak and Kangchendzonga are some of the giants that dominate the horizon. The camp is usually on a grassy flat known as the Green Lake Plain, the name being derived from a small tarn at the eastern end where on a clear morning the reflection of Kangchendzonga is seen in the waters.

(3 to 4 hours)

Rest Day at Green Lakes

Spend the day lazing in the sunshine and watching the peaks. The more intrepid can climb the hill behind the camp for about an hour or so to come to a high point with magnificent views both towards Kangchendzonga as well as down the valley. The Zemu gap that links the Zemu valley to the Talung valley is clearly seen from this high point.

Green Lakes (5050 m) to Yabuk (3850 m)

It is possible to make the march from Green Lakes to Yabuk in one day as the trail is mostly downhill. More intrepid trekkers and porters could try to reach Jakthang on the same day.

(5-6 hours)

Yabuk (3850 m) – Jakthang (3300 m) – Zema (2900 m)

The way down from Yabuk follows the trail through the forest. Zema, which is the road head, can be reached by afternoon and from here it is a short drive back to Lachen.

(5-6 hours)

The trekkers hut at Tsokha

Short Treks/ Day Walks

There are a number of short one day and half day treks in Sikkim which are suitable for visitors who do not have the time to do the longer treks discussed earlier.

Rabongla (2100 m) to Maenam Top (3200 m)

The town of Rabongla is situated on the road to Pemayangste about a three hour drive from Gangtok. The three kilometre steep climb from the town brings the trekker to the hill top of Maenam which towers above the town. The picturesque walk is through the Maenam Wildlife sanctuary; during spring the rhododendron display is quite spectacular. On a clear morning the hill top has a view of the peaks of the Kangchendzonga range.

Damthang(1650 m) to Tendong (2600 m)

Damthang is located fourteen kilometres away from Namchi, the district headquarters of South Sikkim on the Gangtok-Namchi (via Temi) road. The climb to Tendong takes about two hours from Damthang on a trail through the dense forests of the Tendong Sanctuary. Tendong is a fine viewing point: to the east is the Chola peaks, to the west Kangchendzonga and the Singalila range, to the north east can be seen the peaks of the North Sikkim plateau including Gurudongmar.

Hillay (2750 m) to Barsai (3000 m)

The four kilometre walk to the Barsai rhododendron sanctuary passes through forests with a view of the Kangchendzonga peaks in the background. During March and April this part of the trail is ablaze with rhododendron blossoms and it is a delightful day walk with stunning views.

Pemayangtse to Sangacholling Monastery

This is a walk from Pemayangste to Sangacholling following the ridge which joins the two monasteries. The initial walk upto Pelling is flat and on a good day there are brilliant views of the peaks right across the valley. From the Pelling playing field there is a stiff forty five minute climb to Sangacholling. On a clear day the Darjeeling ridge can be seen to the south. To the north is visible all the peaks of the Kangchendzonga range as well as some of the most important monasteries in west Sikkim perched on the hill tops to the north and east, including Khechuperri, Dubdi and Pemayangtse.

White Water Rafting

The Tista and Rangit rivers offer ample opportunities for spectacular white water rafting holidays. The rafting begins at Singtam about an hour's drive from Gangtok and carries on till Tista bazaar about four hours down the river. The rapids, rated according to the Colorado River standards, are grade 2 and 3. It is possible to devise a two day rafting package for US $ 35 per person per day for foreigners and Rs 800 per person per day for Indian tourists. A one day rafting package is also possible.

Rafting on the Tista near Melli, South Sikkim

Chortens and prayer flags at Sangacholling monastery in West Sikkim.

Epilogue

In the spring of 2000 I decided to return to Sikkim. Over the last few years, I had been hearing that Sikkim was now the tourist destination for the twenty-first century. Tourists had been allowed to visit the hitherto restricted north and groups were regularly driving up to Lachung and Yumthang to see the snow in winter and the rhododendrons in spring. The road to the Nathu-La pass in east Sikkim was also open and Indian tourists were driving up to shake hands with Chinese soldiers across the border.

I decided to spend a week in West Sikkim, visiting Pelling, Yoksam, Dzongri and finally returning to the plains via the monastery of Tashiding, which I had visited many years ago. My trekking partner, Srijit Dasgupta, a veteran of many Sikkim visits, decided to take a week off from work and accompany me.

As time was short we hired a Maruti van in Siliguri and drove up to Pelling. With better roads and easier communication it now takes only five hours when it used to take a full day earlier. We crossed the Tista bridge within an hour and

Siniolchu from Rest Camp in the Zemu valley

a half from Siliguri and spotted three rafts careering down the river at an impossible speed. The Tista river was now being used for river rafting expeditions and groups of tourists spend a few days on a rafting adventure through the white waters. At Jorethang, we stopped for lunch at the Namgay Hotel which seemed to have changed little though lots of jeeps and Maruti vans were available outside the hotel to ferry tourists to all parts of the state – Gangtok, Rabang la, Namchi, Dentam, Sombaria, Legship, Gayzing, Tashiding, Yoksam and so on.

At 3 o'clock we drove into Pelling. This sleepy village with a small post office and a couple of houses had changed beyond recognition. Pelling was now firmly on the tourist map of the state. Deepak Pradhan, proprietor of Hotel Kabur, one of the oldest establishments in the village, told me that there were now twenty-three hotels in Pelling. Most of them were concrete two or three storeyed structures with ugly facades in garish colours. In the evening we walked across to the football field below the chorten. Now the new Hindustan Hotel dwarfed the chorten before it and I spotted a Bengali family safe in monkey caps and

anoraks hugging cups of tea on the terrace of the hotel waiting in vain for a view of the mountains. Telephone booths were at every hotel corner and dish antennas connected the visitors to BBC, CNN and Star TV.

The evening remained cloudy as we walked to Pemayangste monastery. I was glad to see that no further construction had been allowed at Pemayangste. The forest below the monastery was as thick and as rich in bird life as it had been before. In the brief half hour we spent there, we spotted blue magpies, tree pies, redstarts and flower peckers. The bird song had not faded.

The next morning we left for Yoksam, the starting point for the Dzongri trek. The trek to Dzongri and beyond to the view point at Goecha La had become one of the most popular for foreign tourists. Jaded with the crowds and tea house trekkers of Nepal, well-heeled foreigners with the seductive dollar were increasingly looking towards Sikkim to provide a once in a lifetime wilderness trekking experience. Danny Denzongpa, the famous Bollywood actor who hails from Yoksam had put up a luxury hotel, the Tashi Gang, where the best comforts were available for these tired and affluent trekkers. Quick to take advantage of the situation, the Sikkim Government had introduced a system of park fees in the Kangchendzonga National Park of which Yoksam was one of the entry points. Indians and foreigners pay the same entry fee of Rs 150 to trek in the Dzongri region. In addition, there are camping fees, fees to use trekking huts, and fees to use a camera as in the Sagarmatha National Park and the Annapurna Conservation Area Project (ACAP) in Nepal. It is now become compulsory for travellers to log in particulars and expected date of return at the local Police Station so that missing trekkers can be located.

On the main street of Yoksam we met a young lad called Pradip Subba, who wanted to be our porter cum guide for the Dzongri trek and we decided to take him along. Over a quick breakfast of omelette and toast at the Wild Orchid Hotel, a humble but homely establishment, we briefed Pradip about our trek and route and asked him to buy some kerosene and provisions from the bazaar. Unlike the tea house treks in Nepal where independent trekkers can make use of lodges to eat and sleep, the trekking huts in Sikkim provide shelter only. Food and provisions including kerosene to cook, stoves etc. have to be carried up from Yoksam making it all the more imperative to have a porter to ferry up the supplies.

The walk from Yoksam to Bakhim had changed little. In 1849, the famous British botanist Sir Joseph Dalton Hooker had walked along the same trail and had commented, "The vegetation consisted of oak, maple, birch, laurel, rhododendron, white daphne, arum, begonias, pepper, fig, wild cinnamon, several epiphytic orchids, vines and ferns in great abundance." The forest was as heavy as before and alive with bird song and waterfalls. There had been little cultivation and the Ratong Chu river roared through the gorge below. We crossed the customary four bridges and arrived at the base of the steep climb to Bakhim about an hour away. Here, camped near the river, we met a group from Tiger Mountain, one of the most reputed trekking companies from Nepal. The group sirdar was from the hill town of Manali in Himachal Pradesh and he was leading a team of British tourists to Dzongri and Goecha La. The team was on their way back and had encountered heavy snow near the pass making the climb difficult for the time of the year.

The next day we started the climb to Dzongri. The trail climbs almost 1250 metres in a time span of around five hours making it the most arduous part of the trek. *Rhododendron arboreum,* one of the most common tree rhododendrons was in bloom until the village of Tsokha, and magnolia, with its' large scented cream blossoms covered whole hillsides with their white and cream flowers. As we climbed higher we noticed that most of the other species of rhododendrons were in bud. 'We are a month too early,' I told Srijit and Pradip agreed.

As we crossed the clearing at Phidang and began the final climb, it began to hail. Even after all these years it still seemed a wild and desolate spot. The air was damp and mountains and mist seemed to hem us in. The hail soon changed to snow. Pradip was walking in slippers and had kept his shoes in his bag in order to protect them from the rain and snow! I asked him if he would make it. He was confident of reaching the Dzongri bungalow and refused to change into his shoes. The wind increased to menacing proportions and drifts of snow began to blow towards us. The shafts of lightning seemed to be answered by crashes of thunder. Our umbrellas provided little protection in the deluge. We crested the ridge at Mon Lepcha to find a few forlorn prayer flags bent in the blizzard. At around three o'clock, caked in snow, we entered the Dzongri hut, relieved to be safe and finally dry. Pradip went and sat near a fire in the chowkidar's quarters while we changed our wet clothes and slipped into warm down sleeping bags.

It snowed for most of the evening and night but a calm and clear morning dawned. In a matter of a few hours spring had given way to winter and the snow lay at least eight inches deep. We decided to walk up to the alp of Dzongri and made our way through the crisp snow. On the alp, next to the yak huts, we found a Japanese group in the process of abandoning camp and proceeding down the Rangit valley. Yaks were being loaded up with tents, stoves, kerosene jerry cans, sleeping bags, duffel bags and food for the downward journey. Sherpas and sirdars monitored operations as camp tables and chairs were packed up and folded away. As we climbed up to the ridge at Dablakhang on the northeastern end of the Dzongri meadow, the weather began to worsen. Ugly storm clouds rushed up the valley and we thought ourselves lucky to catch a glimpse of Pandim, Narsing and Jobonu before they vanished into the mist. Kangchendzonga was already in cloud. Standing next to the four chortens at Dablakhang, where the lamas of Pemayangtse come to pray to the mountains in the monsoon, I felt a sudden desire to see Kangchendzonga again. 'Let's stay another day in Dzongri and try our luck tomorrow,' I said to Srijit.

We spent the day in the Dzongri bungalow. Two groups, French and American, came up and occupied some of the rooms. Unlike us, they had a retinue and their cook was making delicious parathas and pakoras for tea. We cooked plain rice and dal in our pressure cooker and opened a packet of soup for dinner. The weather remained misty and cold and threatened to snow any moment. We resolved to leave at 4.30 am the next morning so that we could reach the chortens in time for the sunrise. I prayed for clear weather that night.

The morning was cold and crisp and the temperature about six degrees below zero when we left the bungalow. As we climbed upto the first ridge there was a magnificent sight of the moon setting over the peaks of the Singalila range, the barrier between Nepal and Sikkim. It's reflected light lit up the Himalayan peaks, Kangchendzonga pale and glowing in it.

Just before leaving for Sikkim I had read in *The Statesman* that for the first time since the successful ascent of Kangchendzonga in 1955 by a British team lead by Charles Evans, the Sikkim Government had allowed a foreign team of mountaineers from Europe to attempt the holy mountain from the Zemu valley in the North. To attempt the mountain by the north east spur is rated by the mountaineer John Hunt as a tougher challenge than Everest. The report mentioned that Wilhelm Bauer, the grandson of the famous Paul Bauer who had led unsuccessful attempts on Kangchendzonga in 1929 and 1931, would be leading a ten-member team to the peak. Lamas all over Sikkim prayed that the expedition to their sacred mountain would be unsuccessful; and sure enough, Bauer had to retreat because of huge avalanches and snow-storms. Vigorous protests from the Buddhists followed, and eventually the government, bowed down to their demands and banned mountaineers from attempting Kangchendzonga as well as some other peaks.

In 1899, the British explorer Douglas Freshfield while making his circuit of Kangchendzonga had seen the mountain from the Onglathang a few hours from Dzongri and had commented:

"What Walter Scott wrote of Melrose Abbey may be applied to Onglathang. Go visit it by pale moonlight. Our moon was almost full. Hidden behind the walls of Jobonu, its orb remained long invisible, and the nearer snows were but faint and indistinct, while between their pale shadowy masses the whole peak of Kangchendzonga was fully illuminated as if by a heavenly searchlight. The rock and ice were transfigured into a silver shrine, a visionary emblem of purity and aspiration. The worship of Kangchendzonga at that moment seemed very reasonable service."

We felt the same way.

To the south a blue haze spread over the plains of India. Pemayangste monastery whose rooftop is visible from Dzongri was also in mist. There was no wind and it was calm and still. In an hour we crested the ridge at Dablakhang once again and this time we were rewarded. After many years, I was greeted with a view of the south face of Kangchendzonga, right across the valley. The satellite peaks of Kabru, Pandim, Narsing and Jobonu completed this dress circle view. The peaks were sparkling with the spring snowfall. Down on the alp of Dzongri the first yaks were slowly being led to pasture, their bells tinkling in the early morning sunshine. Overhead, lammergiers soared looking for prey on the highest peaks. Below us snaking its way through the gorge, was the Prek Chu river that finally joins the Rangit. Free from group-trekkers and tourists who had retreated with the bad weather earlier, the serene beauty of the scene seemed eternal.

We spent an hour on top and then the clouds began to rush in once again.

While I stood near the Dablakhang chortens, I felt sadly certain that it was my farewell trip to the Dzongri alp. In the last twenty-two years I had been in and out of Sikkim; it had almost become my second home. I had visited Dzongri many times. Now that was all going to change.

Within an hour we were on our way to Bakhim. We descended from winter into spring. In the few days that we had been away, some of the primulas had bloomed and their pink blossoms covered rocks and tree trunks. We passed large groups of trekkers on the way to the mountains, kitted out in the best of alpine clothing from premier companies like Berghaus, Mountain Hardware, and Lowe Alpine escorted by their sirdars, cooks, porters and yaks. We began our walk down to Tashiding with heavy hearts.

The next morning, after a quick breakfast at the Bluebird Hotel in Tashiding village run by the Gupta family from the plains of Bihar—we walked up to the monastery. Little seemed to have changed in Tashiding. Tourist traffic seemed to have by-passed one of the most important monasteries in the state. Children played in the courtyard while devout pilgrims muttered their *om mani padme hum* as they did the timeless traditional circuit of the monastery against a backdrop of fluttering prayer flags. This was a reassuringly peaceful Sikkim we could recognize.

After spending a couple of hours at the monastery we walked down to the village. Near the school field, against a backdrop of chortens and prayer flags, I noticed that a cricket match was about to begin. Tashiding was firmly in the grip of cricket fever. The match pitted the village against the monastery. After lunch, we returned a couple of hours later to find the match in the throes of a nail-biting finish. The monastery had to make 116 runs with 8 overs to go, a tall task by any standards. The cries from the fielders and the crowd became more and more vociferous as dusk loomed and the overs dwindled. After a couple of big hits down the Rangit valley, the local incarnation of Sachin Tendulkar was caught at fine leg. He had made a magnificent century before surrendering his wicket. The sky darkened and heavy drops of rain put an end to the match for the day. Neither team had won.

As we walked back to the Bluebird Hotel, I wondered what the future had in store for Sikkim. Educated unemployed youth dominated the villages, looking for livelihoods and outlets for their energy and knowledge. There would have to be a very fine balance between commercialization of Sikkim, that seemed inevitable, and preservation of its environment and culture. The faith of the people in Buddhist rituals and culture was unshakable and I felt this would see them through difficult times, from which the beauty of Sikkim would emerge untarnished.

(Overleaf): Pandim from the Prek Chu valley near Thangsing

Information for Travellers

GETTING THERE

From Calcutta /Delhi
By Air

There is no direct air service to Sikkim. The closest airport is at Bagdogra, 124 km away and about five hours drive from Gangtok. Indian Airlines and Jet Airways both have flights to Bagdogra from Delhi and Calcutta. Sikkim Helicopter Services have introduced a daily helicopter service from Bagdogra airport to Gangtok.

As schedules and fares change frequently, please check with the airlines for current information. Reconfirm all tickets three days in advance.

By Rail

There are a number of overnight trains from Calcutta to Siliguri. The station is at New Jalpaiguri, twenty minutes away by car. The premier train on this route is the Darjeeling Mail. Other trains are the Teesta-Torsa Express, Uttar Banga Express, and Kanchan Kanya Express. All these trains depart from Sealdah station. There are also trains from Delhi to New Jalpaiguri.

By Bus

For budget travellers there are daily overnight 'Rocket' bus services between Calcutta and Siliguri. The buses depart from the Bus Stand at Esplanade near the Shahid Minar. Tickets should be booked in advance. Depending on the condition of the road the journey can take between twelve and sixteen hours. These services should be avoided during the monsoon months due to poor road conditions.

From Nepal/Bhutan

There are no direct flights between Kathmandu and Bagdogra. However, plans are afoot to make Bagdogra an international airport to cater to traffic from Nepal and Thailand. It is however possible to fly from Kathmandu to Biratnagar and drive from there. The distance from Biratnagar to the border Kakarbhitta is about three hours and from there to Siliguri is about an hour. There are night buses from Kathmandu to Karkarbhitta, which take about fifteen hours.

From Bhutan, there are no flights from Paro to Bagdogra. It is possible to drive from Phuntsholing at the southern border to the Coronation Bridge, which joins the road from Siliguri to Gangtok. The journey to the Coronation Bridge would take about three hours. The entire drive from Phuntsholing to Gangtok would take between six to seven hours.

The Road Up
Buses

Sikkim Nationalised Transport (SNT) provides daily services between Siliguri and Gangtok, with a daily direct bus to Bagdogra airport. Passengers arriving i Bagdogra airport can take a taxi c auto-rickshaw to the SNT bu station in Siliguri. Private buses ru throughout the day, often at hourl intervals from the Tenzing Norga Bus stand at Siliguri. There are als frequent buses and taxi service between Darjeeling/Kalimpong an Gangtok.

For trekkers who wish to vis Western Sikkim directly from Siliguri, there are buses and tax from Siliguri to Jorethang in Sout Sikkim. From Jorethang there ar connections by bus/jeep t Gayzing, Pelling and Yoksam vi Tashiding.

Taxis: Maruti vans and car jeeps, and land rovers can be hire from both Siliguri and Bagdogra t Gangtok. It is also possible to get seat on a share taxi. Share taxi usually leave from outside the SN office in Siliguri.

VISAS AND PERMITS

Besides a valid passport (goo for the duration of your stay) an an Indian visa, there are no speci visa requirements. It is advisable t get your Indian visa in your ow home country.

It is now easy to get permi for Sikkim. All Indian Mission abroad are authorised to issue a 15 day inner line permit for Sikkim. Th can be stamped on the passport a

...e time of obtaining the visa for ...dia but one must request it. You ...an also get a 15-day permit from ...ny of the Sikkim Tourism Offices ...cated at Delhi, Calcutta or at ...liguri. The 15-day permit is issued ...n the spot without any delay ...rovided photo copies of passport ...nd visa details along with two ...assport size photographs of the ...plicants are made available then ...nd there.

In case you fail to do this and ...nd yourself at the state border, ...angpo, without a permit, the ...urism Officer stationed there will ...sue a permit with a two-day ...alidity to enable you to enter the ...ate. This permit is then revalidated ...r the full 15 days on arrival at ...angtok. The State Government ...so extends the 15-day permit for ...vo further spells of 15 days at a ...ne in case you wish to stay longer. ...ith the 15-day permit you gain ...ccess to Gangtok, and all district ...eadquarters (Namchi, Gayzing and ...angan) and all sub-divisional ...eadquarters (Soreng, Pakyong, ...bongla) except for Chungthang ...North Sikkim which is accessible ...ly to foreigners who form a group ...four or more persons. This permit ...so covers Rumtek, Phodang, ...emayangste, Khechuperri and ...shiding.

Areas like Tsangu lake which ...a two hour drive from Gangtok, ...e Yumthang Valley in North Sikkim, and the trekking area in West Sikkim are open only to groups of four or more. All this can be arranged through local travel agents on arrival in Sikkim.

CLIMATE

Sikkim has four distinct seasons.

The winter season begins from mid December and lasts until the end of February though in the high altitudes above 3000 m, winter can extend until end April or beginning of May. The alpine regions of Yumthang, Lhonak valley, Dzongri and the Zemu valley sometimes receive snow until early May.

In the valleys, spring comes early sometimes by late February or early March and lasts till mid May. Beginning at the middle elevations, the rhododendrons bloom by mid-March, moving up the hillsides to 3,500 m by mid-May. The orchid season also begins with spring and reaches its peak in April and May. The mountain views tend to get covered by haze by mid May as the days get hotter and the monsoon approaches.

The summer season starts in mid May and carries on till the end of September. From June till September, the monsoon is in full swing and Gangtok receives most of its 325-cm rainfall during this period. The monsoon is not very active in the north; e.g. Muguthang on the Lhonak plateau receives only 60 cm of rain in the year. The monsoon season brings with it roadblocks, landslides and leeches. However, the months of July and August offer the best opportunity to see the high altitude flora at it's best on the alpine meadows.

October to mid- December is autumn and this is one of the finest seasons in Sikkim. The rains have washed the atmosphere clear and there are views of the mountains almost every day. The days are clear and sunny and the nights crisp and cold.

The average summer and winter temperatures in Gangtok are given below:
Summer : Max. 25°C Min. 12°C
Winter : Max. 15°C Min. 5°C

TRAVEL ESSENTIALS

When to Visit

The best season to visit Sikkim is from March to May and again from October to mid December. Autumn is the best time to visit the Himalaya for clear skies and harvest colour. The best season for trekking is from October to mid-December. During spring the rhododendrons and other flora are in full bloom.

Winter is cold at high altitudes with snow above 3000 m and sub-zero temperatures at night. In Gangtok temperatures drop to 5°C (41°F) by mid January. February is often the coldest month and can be wet and blustery.

Clothing

Except for special occasions, dress is informal. The Sikkimese are still quite conservative and especially at the monasteries, women should avoid wearing shorts and skimpy tops; likewise, men should wear trousers and shirts at monasteries. Bring a warm sweater or jacket for mornings and evenings throughout winter and early spring. An umbrella offers the best protection from monsoon rains. In the winter an anorak is often quite useful to wear over a fleece or woollen layer.

Vaccinations

There are no required inoculations for Sikkim. Visitors arriving in India from countries infected by yellow fever must show a certificate of valid yellow fever inoculation. Inoculations against typhoid, hepatitis (gamma globulin), tetanus, polio and meningitis are recommended before coming to India.

Customs

There are no customs formalities specific to Sikkim. Indian customs regulations apply.

CULTURAL CANNINESS

Sikkim, especially rural Sikkim, is still not fully acclimatized to the ways of foreigners, so cultural sensitivity is important when travelling in this land. Keep in mind the following norms, and your chances of inadvertently committing an act of disrespect should be minimized:

• Beggars: don't encourage them. Rather make a donation at the local monasteries or schools that you visit. This will be highly appreciated and the money will be used much more productively!

• Demonstrate respect to sacred places. Don't litter such areas. Avoid stepping or climbing on holy objects. Use all four fingers of the right hand rather than a single finger when pointing to holy sites or people. Try not to touch others or sacred objects with your feet; and

don't point your feet at a person, shrine or a cooking fire. When walking past a chorten or mendang always walk on the left with the chorten on your right.

• Photography : Most people do not mind having their picture taken, but always ask permission before taking pictures - whether it's of people, temples, statues, stupas or lamas. It is usually prohibited to take photographs inside monasteries.

• Gestures : The Indian greeting of Namaste, formally said with palms together in front of the chest, is a polite greeting to people of all faiths. Do not use your left hand while receiving or handing over things, to eat with or to serve food. Do not eat out of common serving dishes or expect others to share food, which you have touched.

MONEY MATTERS

Currency : The Indian rupee (IC stands for Indian currency, R for rupees) is divided into 100 paise. Coins are in denominations of 5,10,25, and 50 paise and 1, 2 and 5 rupees. Notes are in 1, 2, 5, 10, 20, 50, 100 and 500.

Major foreign currencies and travellers cheques can be changed at only those banks, hotels and moneychangers licensed to deal in foreign currency. It is difficult to change money outside Gangtok

You can exchange Indian rupees back into foreign currency upon departure from India, but not to exceed the total amount originally changed. Keep all money exchange receipts to support your re-exchange. Payment for airline tickets must be made in foreign currency. Hotel bills and travel services can be paid in rupees as long as you can show official exchange receipts for the amount.

Credit Cards: Major international credit cards and Indian credit cards are accepted in the larger hotels and a few shops in Gangtok. It is better to come prepared with adequate cash however to avoid problems especially in the smaller towns and in the trekking trails..

Banks : Banks are generally open from 10am to 2pm Monday through Friday, 10am to noon on Saturdays, closed Sundays and government holidays. The State Bank of India can receive telexed money transfers via its central bank, taking up to several days.

Tipping : It is customary to tip about 10 percent in better restaurants, and a few rupees to bellboys or hotel service staff. You need not tip taxi drivers unless you ask them to wait; tipping of long distance taxi or excursion bus drivers is appreciated. Generally, travel and trekking guides receive a greater tip and cooks, porters and staff receive less, depending on their responsibility and performance.

Airport Tax: There is no tax for domestic flights. However, there is a tax for international departures.

IT'S USEFUL TO KNOW....

Hours and Holidays: In Sikkim, government office hours are generally open 10am to 4pm Monday to Saturday. Public holidays coincide with festival days.

Shops are usually open from 10am to 7pm. Most are closed Sundays.

Sunday is the big bazaar day in Gangtok, when farmers and traders sell their goods at Lall Market and it is worth visiting on this day.

Language

English is widely understood throughout the state. Some Nepalese and Sikkimese/Tibetan phrases are also helpful to know, especially when travelling in rural areas:

chaam : *religious masked dances*
chiya: *milk tea*
chorten: *a small Buddhist shrine*
chu: *river*
dhanyabaad/thuche che: *thank you in Nepalese/Sikkimese*
gompa: *a Buddhist monastery*
la : *a mountain pass*
lama: *a Buddhist priest*
Namaste: *the Nepalese greeting*
puja : *ritual offering to the gods*

Electricity and Water: Throughout India, 220-v/50 cycles is used. Electricity is available in all hotels, and even some Trekkers Huts, in Sikkim. There are seasonal water shortages, so do try to conserve water.

Time Differences: Indian Standard Time extends throughout the country. It is 5-1/2 hours ahead of Greenwich Mean Time, 9-1/2 hours ahead of US Eastern Standard Time, and 15 minutes behind Nepal time.

THE LAY OF THE LAND

Airlines

The Indian Airlines booking office is at Tibet Road, Gangtok (Phone: 23099) whereas the Jet Airways booking office is at Mahatma Gandhi Marg, Gangtok. For bookings on the helicopter service between Bagdogra and Gangtok contact RNC Enterprise, Mahatma Gandhi Marg, Gangtok Phone 23556.

Railway Booking Out Agency

At Gangtok, it is located in the premises of Sikkim Nationalized Transport Bus Stand (Phone: 22016) and is open from 10am to 1pm and again from 2pm to 4pm. There are special quotas for trains from New

Jalpaiguri station from this office.

Post & Telegraph Office

The General Post Office is located just after Hotel Tibet on Paljor Stadium Road (Phone: 22385 & 22665). It has STD/ISD & FAX facilities. However, Gangtok and even other towns like Gayzing, Pelling, Singtam, have STD/ISD booths to make long distance calls.

Banks In Gangtok

- Canara Bank.
- State Bank of Sikkim.
- State Bank of India.
- United Commercial Bank.
- Bank of Baroda.
- Central Bank of India.
- Vijaya Bank.

Hospital

- S.T.N.M. Hospital, Stadium Road (Phone: 22059).

Church

- Scottish Mission Church.
- Catholic Church (Phone: 22783).
- Church of North India, below Police Head Quarters.

Hindu Temples

- Thakurbari Temple, Gangtok.
- Sai Baba Mandir, Balwakhani, Gangtok.
- Hanuman Mandir, Hanuman Tok, Gangtok.

Mosque

- Anjuman, below Main Market, Gangtok.

Police

- Sadar Police Station, Tibet Road, Gangtok. (Phone: 100/ 22033).

Shopping

- Old Bazar, Naya Bazar, Super Bazar & Lall Market.

Book Shops

- Citi News Agency, Main Market, Gangtok.
- Jainco, Main Market, Gangtok (Phone: 23774).

GETTING AROUND IN SIKKIM

Taxis and Jeeps: Group jeep taxis run more frequently than buses between major destinations. Unless you book the entire vehicle expect to be squeezed in; try for the front seat which is usually booked in advance. Most of the jeep taxis leave Gangtok in the morning.

In and around Gangtok, taxis do not operate by the meter; most in-city fares run between Rs 20-Rs.50. Maruti cars, vans or jeeps can be hired for day or longer excursions. Some rates for long distances are set, others are negotiable, and a waiting or overnight charge should be paid.

Sightseeing Tours: Sikkim Tourism operates daily sightseeing tours around Gangtok and to more distant sites.

Bicycle Touring: Mountain biking is another way to tour these areas, but only for those in top physical condition. Roads are very steep, ascending and descending thousands of feet between destinations. Traffic is light however and unpaved roads offer some pleasant alternatives. Check with the Tourism offices as to which roads are best and where accommodation is available.

SHOP TILL YOU DROP

A wide variety of handicraft are available for the tourists to take back as Souvenirs, from the Government Institute of Cottage Industries and in many curio shops in Gangtok.

Canvas Wall hanging depicting paintings on different aspects of Sikkim, most of these portray face profiles of tribals, eight lucky signs, dragons, religious processions etc.

Thankas or religious scrolls can also be purchased but these are very expensive.

Choksees are small wooden tables about one and a half to two feet in height with intricate local Tibetan designs on the sides. They are collapsible and can easily be carried.

Tibetan Woollen Carpets are expensive and are adorned with intricate designs and patterns reflecting the art and culture of this state. Brilliant vegetable colour dyes are used for these pure sheep wool carpets.

The exquisitely carved **Dragon Sets** of silver and gold inlaid with precious stones are unique to Sikkim. These consist of finely designed dragons on ear-rings, pendants, finger-rings etc. are either in silver or gold. The craftsmen design the jewellery in such a manner that it looks heavy in weight though they are very light.

Sikkim Tea, which is grown in Temi Tea Estate, is famous the world over and carries a big premium in the world market. Its exotic taste and flavour characterize the tea. It sells by the brand name of 'Solja' and `Kangchendzonga' and is a good idea to carry a few packets back home.

Cardamom or Elachi grows in abundance in Sikkim. A few hundred grams should be purchased.

IN AND AROUND GANGTOK

• **Do-Drul Chorten -** An impressive stupa encircled by prayer wheels. Close by there are two giant statues of the Lord Buddha and Guru Padmasambhava.

• **Institute of Tibetology** - A unique institution, devoted to Tibetology the only one of its kind in the world. On display is perhaps the largest collection of Tibetan artifacts outside Tibet.

• **Tsuklakhang - The Royal Chapel** - The royal chapel, Tsuklakhang, is within the palace grounds. It is the principal place of worship and assembly and the repository of a vast collection of Buddhist scriptures.

• **Enchey Monastery -** Surrounded by prayer flags and overlooking Gangtok, this 19th century Nyingma pa gompa is a haven of tranquillity.

• **Deer Park -** This park located adjacent to Tashiling (The Secretariat) houses a statue of the Buddha, similar to the one in Bodhgaya. There are wide enclosures for deer and a number of local animals, such as the Red Panda, are housed in cages on these grounds.

• **White Hall -** This was built in 1932 in memory of the first Political Officer of Sikkim, Claude White. There is an Officers Club and a badminton court in the White Hall.

• **The Ridge** is a small stretch of plain and flat road above the town of Gangtok. It is just about five minutes walk from the main market. The Ridge has the White Hall and the Chief Minister's official residence on one end and the beautifully designed Palace Gates on the other. The ridge is lined with plants and trees when in bloom are a riot of colour. Flower shows, which attract tourists from all over the world, are held just below the Ridge.

• **Tashi View Point -** Worth visiting in pre-dawn hours to catch the awe-inspiring sight of the sun rising on the snow capped peaks of the Kangchendzonga range.

• **Hanuman Tok -** A short uphill walk from the town centre gets you to this unpretentious mandir and splendid photography point.

• **Ipecac Gardens -** These botanical gardens dedicated to the nurture and display of the flora of Sikkim is an ideal picnic spot.

• **Bul Buley -** Encompassing an area of 205 hectares is this Himalayan Zoological Park.

• **Cottage Industries -** The best place to pick up local handicrafts. You may also see the artisans at work.

• **Tsangu Lake -** With an average depth of 50 ft, this spectacular lake is situated 35km from Gangtok at an altitude of 3,600 m on the Gangtok - Nathu-la highway. The road with an awesome precipice on one side takes you through the Kyongnosla Alpine Sanctuary.

• **Menmecho Lake** lies 20 km ahead of Tsangu lake, cradled between the mountains below Jelep la pass, is the source of river Ranpochu that meets Tista at Rangpo. It is rich in trout. A dak bungalow and a tourist lodge is available for overnight stay.

• **Rumtek** A drive through the picturesque terraced rice fields will bring you to the headquarters of the Dharma Chakra Centre, the present seat of His Holiness, the Gyalwa Karmapa, head of the Kargyupa Sect.

• **Kabi Longstok** 25 km from Gangtok, just before Phodong is Kabi Longstok. There is a spot amidst tall trees, where the treaty of brotherhood between the Lepcha Chieftan-Thekung Tek and the Tibetan Chief Khye Bhumsa was signed.

Accommodation in Gangtok
There are plenty of hotels and lodges in Gangtok to suit all budgets. However, you'd be well advised to check for heating and hot water in winter. Low season discounts can be availed between January and March and July and August. Some of the hotels are listed below:

Hotel Norkhill
Paljor Stadium Road, Gangtok.
Tel: 23186, 23187, Fax: 25369

Hotel Tashi Delek
Mahatma Gandhi Marg, Gangtok.
Tel: 22991, 222038, 24155
Fax: 22362

Trekking Gear
• Walking boots
• Rucksack
• Sleeping bag
• Warm jacket (Down jacket will be preferred if you plan to go above 4000 m)
• 2 pairs of underwear
• 2 pairs of walking socks
• 2 pairs of sports shirts / warm long sleeved shirt
• 1 pair thermal underwear
• Long trousers for walking (or long skirt for women)
• 2 cotton T-shirts
• Gloves
• Warm hat which covers your ears (for above 4000 m)
• Sunglasses (vital for the snow)
• Sunblock cream
• Soap and soap dish
• Small towel
• Toothbrush and toothpaste
• Personal first aid kit
• Sheet of plastic (For if it rains)
• 1 roll of toilet paper.
• 2 large plastic bags (One for smelly clothes, one for things which must be kept dry)
• Plastic mug
• Torch
• Waterbottle
• Iodine tablets
• Umbrella

E- mail: tashidelek@sikkim.org
Web: www.hoteltashidelek.com

Hotel Tibet
Paljor Stadium Road, Gangtok.
Tel: 22527, 23468; Fax: 26233
E-mail: hotel.tibet@gokulnet.com

Central Hotel
31A, National Highway, Gangtok.
Tel: 22105, 22553, 23573;
Fax: 22240
E-mail: central.hotel@gokulnet.com
or hotel.central@hotmail.com

Norbugang Hotel
Paljor Stadium Road, Gangtok.
Tel: 22237/23537

The Chumbi Residency
Tibet Road Gangtok.
Tel: 23999, 26618   Fax: 22707.

Hotel Anola
Mahatma Gandhi Marg, Gangtok
Tel : 24233/23238 Fax : -24976
E-mail : anola@mailcity.com

Hotel Himalchuli
31-A National, Zero Point
Post Box # 56 Gangtok.
Tel : 24643
E-mail : himalchuli@usa.net

Hotel Golden Pagoda
Mahatma Gandhi Marg, Gangtok.
Tel: 26928, 26929.
E-mail:
goldenpagoda@hotmail.com

Hotel Mist Tree Mountain
Hospital Point, Paljor Stadium Road, Gangtok.

el: 23827, 24263 Fax : 26339.
- mail: nirmal_mist@hotmail.com

IKKIM TOURISM FFICES

ourist Information Centre,
Mahatma Gandhi Marg, Gangtok.
el: (03592)-25277/ 22064
ax: (03592)- 25647

ikkim Tourist Information
entre,
ikkim Nationalised Transport
olony,
ill Cart Road, Siliguri.
el: 432646

ikkim Tourist Information
ounter,
agdogra Airport,
agdogra.

ikkim Tourist Information
entre,
C Poonam Building,
/2 Russell Street,
alcutta.
el: (033)-2468983/ 2451960/
294577 /2469786

ikkim Tourist Information Centre,
lew Sikkim House,
, Panchsheel Marg,
hanakyapuri,
lew Delhi.
el: (011)-6115346

Travel Agents in Sikkim

Most of the travel companies listed below organise group treks, white water rafting, monastic and cultural tours, and mountain biking. Some of these companies are also engaged in speciality tours like birding and alpine flora and fauna tours.

1. Sikkim Trekking and Travel Services Pvt. Ltd.
P.O. Box 132, Gangtok 737 101, India
Tel: +(91)-(3592)-23797 Fax: +(91)-(3592)-22707   E-mail: dorjee@dte.vsnl.net.in

2. Namgyal Treks & Tours
P.O. Box #.75, Tibet Road, Gangtok 737 101, India
Tel: +(91)-(3592)-23701/27027/ 24924 Fax: +(91)-(3592)-23067; E-mail: trekking@dte.vsnl.net.in

3. Potala Tours & Treks
 Paljor Stadium Road, Gangtok 737 101, India
Tel: +(91)-(3592)-22041/24434/ 26934 Fax: +(91)-(3592)-22707; E-mail: potala@dte.vsnl.net.in

4. Sikkim Tours and Travels Pvt. Ltd.
Post Box: 155 GPO, Church Road, Gangtok 737101, India
Tel: +(91)-(3592)-22188 Fax: +(91)-(3592)-27191   E-mail: sikkimtours@sikkim.org
or sikkimtours@yahoo.co.uk
or lukendra@yahoo.co.uk

5. Singalila Tours and Treks
31-A National Highway, Gangtok 737 101, India
Tel: +(91)-(3592)-24643 Fax: +(91)-(3592)-22707; E-mail: singalilatreks@mailcity.com

6. Siniolchu Tours & Travels
Paljor Stadium Road, Gangtok 737 101, India
Tel : 25569/24572/24582
Fax : 26068/22707.
E-mail: siniolchu@dte.vsnl.net.in

7.Yak & Yeti Travels, Sikkim
31-A, National Highway, Zero Point, Gangtok 737 101, India
Tel: +(91)-(3592)-24643 Fax: +(91)-(3592)-24643;
E-mail: yakyeti@lycos.com or yakyeti@sikkim.org

8. Tashila Tours and Travels
31-A National Highway Gangtok 737101, Sikkim, India
Tel : +(91)-(3592)-22979/22206/ 23759 Fax : 01-3592-22155
E-mail: tashila@sikkim.org

9. Yuksom Tours & Treks
Borong House, Gangtok 737 001, India
Tel: +(91)-(3592)-23473/26822
Fax: +(91)-(3592)-22707; E-mail: takapa@dte.vsnl.net.in

154

SELECTED READING

Tours in Sikkim and Darjeeling District
Percy Brown

Sikkim
P.N.Chopra

Land of the Thunderbolt
Earl of Ronaldshay

Folk Lore and Customs of the Lepchas of Sikkim
Stock de Beauvior

Smash and Grab: Annexation of Sikkim
Sunanda K Datta Ray

Round Kangchenjunga
Douglas Freshfield

Himalayan Village - An Account of the Lepchas of Sikkim
Geoffrey Gorer

Himalayan Journals
Sir Joseph Dalton Hooker

Rhododendrons of the Sikkim Himalaya
Sir Joseph Dalton Hooker

Touring in Sikkim and Tibet
David Macdonald

Sikkim
P.Mele and Desmond Doig

Living with Lepchas
J. Morris

Sikkim and the Tibetan Frontier
Colman Macaulay

The Way and the Mountain
Marco Pallis

The Gazetteer of Sikkim
H. Risley

Mountain Top Kingdom - Sikkim
C.Y. Salisbury and A. Kendall

The Lepchas, Culture and Religion of a Himalayan People
H. Siiger

Travels in Nepal and Sikkim
Richard Temple

Among the Himalayas
A. Wadell

Lamaism in Sikkim
A. Wadell

Sikkim and Bhutan
Claude White

Sikkim
Rajesh Bedi, Asha Rani Mathur and Puspesh Pant

Enchanted Frontiers
Nari Rustomji

The Butterflies of Sikkim Himalayas
Meena Haribal

Sikkim, Darjeeling and Bhutan
Rajesh Verma

The Sikkim Saga
B.S.Das

The Birds of Sikkim
Salim Ali

Trekking in Pakistan and India
Hugh Swift

Sikkim-Himalayan Rhododendrons
Udai Pradhan and Sonam Lachungpa

Kangchenjunga Challenge
Paul Bauer

The Kangchenjunga Adventure
Frank Smythe

Sikkim, Darjeeling and Kalimpong
Wendy Brewer Lama

Sikkim Coronation
Coronation Souvenir Book Committee

PHOTOGRAPHY CREDITS

GLOSSARY

This glossary has been compiled from the common terms found in the different languages used in Sikkim.

Asek: Lepcha betrothal ceremony

bazaar, bazar: market place

baksheesh: tip

bhailo: song sung by Nepali girls visiting houses in-groups during Tihar

bhat: cooked rice

boku: Bhutia gown

bon: the animist pre-Buddhist religion of the Lepchas

Brahmins: the priestly cast of the Hindus

cairns: pile of stones to mark a pass or a trail

chhang: Tibetan millet beer

chappati: flat unleavened bread also called roti

chi: Lepcha millet beer

Chho: lake

chu: river

Chhetri: warrior caste

choktse: small painted wooded table crafted by Bhutias

chowkidar: custodian of a bungalow

chorten: a small wayside Buddhist shrine found on the trail

choubandi: double-breasted blouse worn by Nepali women

chura: silver bracelets worn by Nepali women

churpi: cheese made from yak milk

dak bungalow: Rest House usually Government owned

dal: lentil soup, usually eaten with rice

damaru: big drums

dewsi: traditional songs sung by groups of Nepali boys visiting houses in the neighbourhood during Bhai Tika and Tihar

doko: cane basket carried by porters

dudh: milk

durbar: palace

dzong: fort or palace

gada: traditional Lepcha dress for males, consisting of a long piece of striped cloth worn loosely down to the knee.

gaon: village

ghar: house

gunui: skirt worn by Nepali women reaching down to the ankles and with very small pleats at the front

gompa: Buddhist monastery

Guru Rimpoche: founder of Tibetan Buddhism also called Guru Padmasambhava

haat: market

himal: mountain

honju: long-sleeved blouse worn by Bhutia women

jhankari: tribal priests of the Nepalese

karma: sum of ones good and bad actions

khada: ceremonial scarf

khukri: tool used by Nepalese to cut wood and split bamboo

khola: small river

la: mountain pass

lama: Buddhist priest

lakhang: small wayside place of worship

Losar: Tibetan New Year

Loosong: Sikkimese New Year

maidan: broad grassy meadow

Mandal: hereditary office among Lepchas for collection of revenue

mandala: model representing the entire cosmos placed at the altar in Buddhist monasteries

mandir: temple

mani stone: stone carved with Buddhist chant 'Om mani padme hum'

mani wall: wall built of mani stones in hill country

mantra: prayer chant

mela: country fair

moong: Lepcha evil spirit

momo: steamed or fried dumplings

mun: Lepcha priest who is supposed to be possessed and able to ward off illness and misfortune caused by evil spirits

nadi: small stream or river

namaste: Nepali greeting

nagare: kettle drum

Nyingma-pa: one of the Red Hat sects of Tibetan Buddhism

Om mani padme hum: Buddhist mantra that roughly translates into 'hail to the jewel in the lotus'

pak-doong: trumpet

panchayat: village democracy

parbat: mountain

pangden: striped apron worn by married Bhutia women

phipon: village headman in Lachen and Lachung

pipsey: thin bamboo straw used to drink chhang

puja: religious rite

pundits: Indians who were secretly sent by the British to survey Tibet

rakshi: distilled spirits made from grain

roti: bread

rimpoche: reincarnate lama

sadhu: wandering Hindu holy man

sangha: order of monks started by Gautama Buddha

salwar: pantaloons

sirdar: head porter or leader of the trek

thangka, thanka: sacred painting on canvas framed with brocade

topi: Nepali hat

tsampa: roasted barley flour, a staple food among the yak herdsmen.

tulkus: high lamas of the Kargyupa sect

stupa: hemispherical Buddhist shrine

yak: main beast of burden for carrying loads in the high mountains

yeti: the mythical anthropoid, also know as the Abominable Snowman

zopkiok, zopkio : a hybrid bull, the cross between a yak and a cow

ACKNOWLEDGMENTS

This book is in essence a collaborative effort that has involved many people over several years. I owe most to my long-time friend and trekking partner Srijit Dasgupta who accompanied me on many of my visits to Sikkim. We spent a long time together photographing in Sikkim, selecting the photographs, planning this book and finally editing the proofs and layout. His contribution to this project has been invaluable.

I am particularly grateful to Bunny Gupta for her unstinted support and deep knowledge of Sikkimese history and culture. In many ways, she is the architect of this book. I would also like to acknowledge the contribution made by the late Dilip Gupta without whom this book would not have been possible.

I am extremely grateful to Anuradha Roy who edited this book with great attention, and Neelima Rao, who is responsible for the innovative layout, as well as assistance with selecting photographs. I thank them both for their matchless support and guidance.

The Densapa family in Gangtok, particularly Jigdal and Thinlay Densapa deserve special thanks for making it possible for me to travel to many parts of Sikkim. Their Cherry Banks residence was like a home for me in Sikkim, the memory of which I will always treasure.

I would like to thank Lt General J. K. Puri, Major General Kukreti, Brigadier Sidhu, Brigadier Pranab Dutt, Brigadier D. R. Sehgal, Major K. H. Singh, Major B. V. Naresh, Major Thapa and the other officers and jawans of 17 Assam Rifles and 112 Mountain Brigade for their hospitality during my journeys in North Sikkim. Without them, many of the treks which I undertook, especially to the Lhonak valley and the North Sikkim plateau would not have been possible.

Karma Topden, once Secretary to the Chief Minister, was my introduction to Sikkim and his assistance in the early days of the project was invaluable; Karma Gyatso, then District Collector, North Sikkim, very kindly provided me with the necessary infrastructural support for my trip to Dzongu in the North district; A. Ghatak, IPS, then Inspector General of Police, Government of Sikkim, was an immense help in myriad ways. I gratefully acknowledge these debts.

While travelling in Sikkim I received more help and assistance that can be acknowledged individually and I would like to thank all those who opened their homes to me and were more helpful and hospitable than I ever expected. Special thanks to L. S. Wangyal and N. D. Das of Gayzing, Yap Phuchung and Sonam of Yoksam, T. P.Ghimiray, then District Collector of West Sikkim, Tseten Baro, General Manager of Hotel Tibet, Gangtok and the management and staff of Hotel No Name, Gayzing.

Durga Das Pradhan of Das Studio, Darjeeling and Prosenjit Dasgupta provided me with the photographs of the fauna of Sikkim which I did not have. I am extremely grateful to both of them. I am also indebted to Dr Keith Sprigg for his assistance with the history and culture of the Lepchas and Wangchuk Basi of Kalimpong for his contribution to some of the research for this book. I would like to thank Dipankar Bir for his excellent duplication of all the images that appear in this book. A special thanks to Indira Gongba, formerly of Summit Tours Darjeeling, who is now based in New York, for planning and organising a number of my treks in the high Himalaya. Her support from Darjeeling was something I had come to depend upon during the Sikkim years.

I would like to acknowledge the support I received from Pratap Gupta, Radharani Mitra, Debapriya Dam, Atanu Ray, Arup Das, and the Das family of 172 Jor Bagh, New Delhi.

And finally, I must thank Ronnie Pillai for having faith in my work and supporting this project right from the beginning when it had seemed suspiciously like a pipe dream.

Sujoy Das
November 2000
Calcutta